best sex writing
2012

best sex writing
2012

Rachel Kramer Bussel

Edited by
Rachel Kramer Bussel

Guest Judge
Susie Bright

CLEiS
PRESS

Published in the United States by Cleis Press Inc.,
2246 Sixth Street, Berkeley CA 94710.

Printed in the United States.
Cover design: Scott Idleman
Cover photograph: idon/Getty Images
Text design: Frank Wiedemann
First Edition.
10 9 8 7 6 5 4 3 2 1

Trade paper ISBN: 978-1-57344-759-1
E-book ISBN: 978-1-57344-771-3

Reprint acknowledgments appear on page 209.

Library of Congress Cataloging-in-Publication Data

Best sex writing 2012 / edited by Rachel Kramer Bussel ; Susie Bright, guest judge.
-- 1st ed.
    p. cm.
  ISBN 978-1-57344-759-1 (pbk. : alk. paper)
1. Sex--United States. I. Bussel, Rachel Kramer. II. Title: Best sex writing.

HQ18.U5B45 2012
306.70973--dc23

                                    2011044554

CONTENTS

When the Sex Guru Met the Sex Panic
Susie Bright

I learned everything I know about "Best of" annual collections from Mrs. Hogan, my second-grade elementary school teacher. Mrs. Hogan was a believer in The Great Beyond. Each year, she led her class to prepare a time capsule containing everything that was important in our human calendar, a Tupperware bucket filled with news clippings, snapshots, Matchbox cars, dolls in the latest outfits.

We buried our historic treasure in the back forty of our school's playing fields, our mark upon the world. Mrs. Hogan promised that in the decades to come our descendants—and better yet, "visitors from universes we can't imagine!"—would discover our time capsule and learn intimately how we odd little creatures once lived.

What would intelligent life have to say if it came upon a volume of *Best Sex Writing 2012*, a montage of American sexual lives and morés? I can sense the Martian trembling, the Venusian arching an eyebrow. Was our species trying to extinguish itself with puritanical wrath—or just squeeze out one last ecstatic pop shot? What a terrible struggle between the two.

On one side of the current sex news we have the orgasm guru, the pleasure benefactor, the inspirational bohemian. In these stories you'll find some of the clearest voices of human connection, of genuine delight in the possibilities of sexual creativity. The writers of these pieces describe an erotic identity unfettered by shame, a marvel in all its variety, the authentic glue that keeps us going, both literally and philosophically.

The other side of the newsmakers are just as interested in sex, even obsessed by it. But their object is panic. The fearmongers of our 21st-century Gilded Age are fanatical about social control through sex, largely using women and young people as bait.

Not only are there fewer jobs in America in 2012, not only is there less economic parity, less care for the weakest and most vulnerable, but according to the fundamentalist pundits there is also a run on virtue. By their lights, America is losing its imperial power because so many of its citizens are so terribly naughty and aren't receiving their proper punishment.

If anyone cares to rip back the curtains on the panicmongers' lurid accusations—as many of the writers here do—they'll find that the sex panics are falsehoods, divisions that thrive and multiply on a lack of democracy and sunshine. Women are not "born" to be vestal virgins or wretched harlots (thereafter saved or punished). Sexual dialogue is not obscene. Gender identity and sexual attractions are not cribbed from a cooked-up Bible story. Our sex lives are, to put it humbly, our humanity—not something to be destroyed with pharmaceutical or prison profit schemes, or made into target practice by election-scoring vendetta seekers.

What I find strange is that the very people who want sexual access and freedom denied to others are living high on the hog themselves. It's a harlot's secret: the panicmongers are always revealed to be some of the kinkiest people around—they have "sex on the brain," as my old schoolteacher would have said. It turns out that Mr. Punisher and Mrs. Slutshamer are themselves terribly interested in how to have a shocking blue orgasm, how to feel sublime in their bodies, how to connect with the most awesome erotic possibility of their lives. They want it bad—they pay for it, they seek it out. They simply don't feel that anyone else can have the same desire and self-determination without being a threat to them on their tenuous throne.

A good friend of mine works as a dominatrix in Texas. After a recent shitstorm of sex-negativity in her state, she sent me an indignant letter in which she wrote: "Susie, I'm not spanking any more Republicans. I've had it."

I wrote her back: "I fear you will starve."

I made her laugh, but I share her outrage. We both know it's not one political party, or a few bad apples, but rather a massive, nation-level betrayal of civil rights, of freedom of speech, of the American dream—wide open spaces, great educations, and sexual freedom be damned.

I hope this collection lights a fire in your belly. There *are* chapters here that will bring you respite, some mischievous inspiration, or silky nostalgia. But in the main, we're here to reveal the well-sharpened pitchforks of sexual hypocrisy. The reporting is excellent, the exposés jaw-dropping. These writers are activists as well as dreamers. They know in their bones, cocks, and clits that the consequence of sexual fearmongering is a barren world that not even the most deluded prig would want to live in.

Susie Bright
Santa Cruz
November 2011

Beyond the Headlines: Real Sex Secrets
Rachel Kramer Bussel

I think about sex a lot—every day, in fact. I don't mean that in an "I want to get it on" way, but in a "What are other people up to?" way. I'm a voyeur, first and foremost, and this extends to my writing. I'm naturally curious about what other people think about sex, from their intimate lives to how their sexuality translates to the larger world.

With the Best Sex Writing series, I get to merge my voyeuristic self with my journalism leanings, and peek into the lives, public and private, of those around me. This volume in the series doesn't pull any punches; the authors have strong opinions, whether it's Marty Klein sticking up for circumcision in the face of an effort in California to criminalize it, Roxane Gay taking the *New York Times* to task for its treatment of an 11-year-old rape victim, Thomas Roche calling out *Newsweek* for its shoddy reporting about prostitution, or Radley Balko examining a child pornography charge.

There are also more personal takes on sex here that go beyond facile headlines or easy answers, that aren't about making a point so much as exploring what real-life sex is like in all its beauty, drama, and messiness. Whether it's Amber Dawn and Tracy Quan sharing the truth about their lives as sex workers, or Hugo Schwyzer explaining the damage our culture does to men with its mythology about their innate sexual prowess, or Tim Elhajj's first-person account of pre—don't ask, don't tell military life, these authors show you a side of sex that you rarely see.

What you are about to read are stories, all true, some reported on the streets and some recorded from lived experience, from the front lines of sexuality. They deal with topics you read about in the headlines, and some topics you may never have considered. They are but a small sampling of the many kinds of sexual stories I received in the submission process.

Part of why I think sex never goes out of style, as a topic or activity, is that it is so very complex. There is no one way to do it, nor two, nor three. Sex can be mundane or mind-blowing, and for those who are trying to get from the former to the latter, there is a plethora of resources but also a host of misinformation purveyed by snake oil salesmen.

In *Best Sex Writing 2012*, you will read about subjects as diverse as "Guys Who Like Fat Chicks," the care and handling of a man's penis, and the glamour and glitter of the Latina drag world. Abby Tallmer, telling a story set in a very specific time and place—the gay leather clubs of New York's Meatpacking District in the 1990s—manages to capture why sexual community is so vital. Tallmer writes, "These clubs gave us a place to feel that we were no longer outsiders—or rather, they made us feel that it was better to be outsiders, together, than to force ourselves to be just like everybody else."

I'm especially pleased to present stories about the kinds of sexuality and sexual issues that don't always make the headlines, from Lynn Harris's investigation of dating with an STD to Hugo Schwyzer's moving look at men's need to be sexually desired and what happens when boys and men are told that wanting to be desired is wrong. Joan Price gives some insight into elder sexuality, as well as into what it's like to purchase the services of a sexual healer. The topic of elder sex is often treated with horror or disgust, or the focus is placed on concern over STDs—which is a worthy topic this series has explored before. But Price, author of two books on elder sexuality (her piece here is excerpted from *Naked At Our Age*), obliges the reader to see the humanity behind her age. She writes, "My birthday erotic massage from a gentle stranger changed something in me. It showed me that I was still a responsive, fully sexual woman, getting ready to emerge from the cocoon of mourning into re-experiencing life. I realized that one big reason I ended up on Sunyata's massage table was so that I could get ready to reenter the world."

Not all, or even most, of the reading here is "easy." Much of it is challenging and heartbreaking. Roxane Gay's media criticism centers on a *New York Times* story about a Texas gang rape and why "The Careless Language of Sexual Violence" distorts our understanding about rape. You may think such a piece doesn't belong in an anthology with this title, but until we rid our world of sexual violence so that everyone can freely express themselves sexually, we need to hear searing indictments of media or those in power who ignore injustice.

As an editor, I'm not only looking for pieces that I agree with, or identify with, but for work that illuminates something new about a topic that's been around forever. The authors here dig deep, challenging both mainstream ideas about sex and a few sex-positive sacred cows. Ellen Friedrichs sticks up for the right of teenagers to be sexual without throwing parents, school boards, and other adults into a sex panic. Amanda Marcotte explores the fast-moving SlutWalk protest phenomenon, which has garnered criticisms from various sides, from being futile to only appealing to white women.

I will quote Abby Tallmer again, because I don't hear the words "sexual liberation" often enough these days. What moves me most about her piece is that you don't have to be a New Yorker, queer, leather, or kinky to understand what she's talking about. I'm 100 percent with her when she writes, "Back then, many of us believed that gay liberation was rooted in sexual liberation, and we believed that liberation was rooted in the right—no, the need—to claim ownership of our bodies, to experience and celebrate sexuality in as many forms as possible, limited only by our time and imagination." I hope this applies in 2012 just as much as it did in the 1970s, 80s, or 90s.

The truth is, I could have filled a book twice this size. Every day, stories are breaking, and being told, about sex—some wondrous, some heartbreaking. This is not a one-handed read, but it is a book that will stimulate your largest sex organ: your brain. Whether you live and breathe sex, you are curious about sex, or somewhere in between, I hope *Best Sex Writing 2012* informs, incites, and inspires you. I hope it inspires you to write and tell your own sexual story, because I believe the more we talk about the many ways sex moves us, the more we work toward a world where sexual shame, ignorance, homophobia, and violence are diminished.

I'd love to hear your thoughts about this book and what you think are the hot topics around sex. Feel free to email me at rachel@bestsexwriting.com with your comments and suggestions for next year's anthology.

Rachel Kramer Bussel
New York
November 2011

Sluts, Walking
Amanda Marcotte

Toronto police officer Michael Sanguinetti probably thought of himself as a noble warrior against the arbiters of political correctness when he claimed, at a crime safety seminar at Osgoode Hall Law School, that the key to keeping men from raping you is to "avoid dressing like sluts." But what he actually ended up doing was putting the final nail in the coffin of the narrative of the "humorless feminist" vs. the yuk-yuking sexists who have a monopoly on the funny. A group of men and women who were outraged at this supposed rape prevention advice responded by organizing a protest march to the front doors of the Toronto Police Service, and with a cheeky nod to Sanguinetti's comment, called the whole thing "SlutWalk." They also encouraged attendees to dress however they liked, including in all sorts of clothes that are commonly understood to be "slutty," in order to drive home the point that clothes don't cause rape—rapists do. The idea was to fight hate with humor, and fight violence with cheek and irony.

Organizers certainly wanted attention, but they probably didn't have any idea what kind of attention the concept of sluts walking would get. In retrospect, the subsequent media blitz should have been predictable. The word *slut* probably generates more click-throughs than any other word on the Internet, after all, and the idea of sluts marching in protest, instead of simply sucking and fucking away in their relegated role as fantastical creatures of the pornographic imagination, was shocking enough that people simply couldn't stop talking about it. Clearly there was a strong need to remind people that because a woman may want to have sex with some people doesn't mean she has to take all comers—so international SlutWalk was born. SlutWalks were conducted in LA, Boston, Brisbane, Amsterdam, São Paulo, London, Helsinki, Buenos Aires, Berlin, and Cape Town, just to name a few. Women all over the world wanted to say they had a right to wear what they want and go out if they want without giving carte blanche to rapists to assault them.

Making the movement international was helped in part because the message of SlutWalk is straightforward. It's an update on the Take Back the Night rallies. Back when those were formed, feminists were saying, "Hey, we should be able to leave our houses after dark without getting raped." Now we're adding to that list a few other things we should be able to do without some dude raping us and having people excuse it as if rapists were a kind of vigilante police force assigned to the task of keeping bitches in line: wear what we want, go to parties, have as many sexual partners as we like, drink alcohol. Eventually we plan to reach a point where women enjoy the freedom of men to do what they like without the inference that you have it coming if someone rapes you.

SlutWalk drew the inevitable controversy that attends women saying they have a right to do what they want without being punished for it by the traditional methods of putting women in their place, such as forced childbirth or being mauled by rapists. Certainly, right wing responses to SlutWalk were predictable for this. The right-wing ethos is to demand that women's sexuality and social lives be constrained with the threat of unwanted childbearing, STDs, and sexual abuse, and therefore they quite predictably defend abortion regulations, anticontraception propaganda in schools, men who catcall women on the streets, and defense attorneys who use the "she was asking for it" tactic to get their rapist clients off the hook. The predictability of these right-wing responses relegated them to background noise, no more worth debating than that grass remains green and the sky remains blue.

No, what distressed SlutWalk supporters was the noise from feminists denouncing the effort, primarily on the basis of a profound misunderstanding of the use of the word *slut*. For some reason, critics got it in their head that SlutWalk was about reclaiming the word *slut*, though their refusal to hear participants who denied that there was any kind of reclamation project going on inclines me to think they just wanted to get angry that young women were wearing miniskirts without apology.

Antipornography activists Gail Dines and Wendy Murphy were by far the most egregious offenders when it came to stubbornly refusing to get it. They argued against SlutWalk in the *Guardian,* writing, "Encouraging women to be even more 'sluttish' will not change this ugly reality. As teachers who travel around the country speaking about sexual violence, pornography and feminism, we hear stories from women students who feel intense pressure to be sexually available 'on demand.'"

It was a mind-boggling exercise in arguing with a straw man. SlutWalk is not saying, "Everyone has to be exactly the same: dress in nothing and have sex with everyone who asks." Slut-Walk is saying, "Even if you think someone's a slut, don't rape her." In fact, a protest against the consensus that it's OK to rape a woman just because of what she's wearing is a protest against the expectation that women be available on demand. Murphy and Dines might as well have argued that people protesting police brutality were supporting it by encouraging folks to believe they have a right to a life fuller than sitting quietly at home in fear of the police.

Dines reinforced the sense that she objected to SlutWalk precisely because she wants young women to feel shame for being sexy when she went on the BBC's "World Have Your Say" and practically hyperventilated while describing young women who walk around wearing tight, low-cut jeans and skimpy shirts as if they had every right in the world to wear what they want. (Hint: They do, and men shouldn't rape them for it.) Dines's argument skews very close to the conservative argument that women's sexuality and sexual freedom must be curtailed for the good of civilization. She argues that women need to rein it in so that other women don't feel they have to be sexual to get men's attention. This is scarcely different from the conservative argument that the "hookup culture" is making it so easy for men to get laid that they won't give women what they really want, which is marriage. If for "marriage" you substitute "respect" or "not bugging you for sex" it's functionally the same argument.

It was particularly strange for Dines to hook her hostility toward sexual playfulness in the public space to SlutWalk, since SlutWalk objectively did not pressure women to tart it up for dudely enjoyment. SlutWalk organizers encouraged women to wear whatever they wanted, anything from their sluttiest outfit to complete coverage in head-to-toe cloth. Katha Pollitt, writing for *The Nation*, captured the spirit perfectly when she said that Slut-Walkers were "attacking the very division of women into good girls and bad ones, Madonnas and whores."

Why, then, did so many participants find it useful to walk dressed in the traditional garb of the slut, the miniskirt and the fishnet? Because they were challenging the retort to women who dress in revealing clothes, which is that they're somehow sending A Message to men. The exact content of this Message is rarely spelled out by people who are concerned about it; it is instead expressed as "What do you expect men to think if you leave the house looking like that?"

Here's what I expect:

If I'm out on the town wearing a cute minidress, I expect that I'll get a lot of indifference, some men thinking I look good, some men thinking that I want to be attractive, some men thinking I enjoy feeling sexy, some men flirting—and some men thinking, "I wouldn't wear those shoes with that dress." I expect men to be happy they live in a world where people have fun and exude sexual energy, because I believe sex is pleasurable and good and that a little more sexual energy in the world tends to improve the fun we have at home.

What I don't expect men to think is *Oh boy, I get to rape that one!* or *Clearly, she forfeited her right not to be harassed when she broke the nonexistent rule about skirt length written by me.* I feel that these are reasonable expectations, since the indifferent or favorable re-actions I described above are what happens to me 99 percent of the time when I wear a minidress in public.

I expect that when a man thinks a woman being sexy means

that she isn't smart or deserving of basic respect, you know everything you need to know about him, and he is the one who has forfeited his right to be treated with respect, not the woman he claims provoked him. I think such a man doesn't actually respect any women; he's just making excuses because he likes harassing women. I expect other people not to make excuses or consider his opinion to matter in any way. I expect instead that such men be shunned by decent people.

I expect when I use the word *slut* in an arch, ironic way that men will find it both funny and insightful. I expect men to understand humor. I expect men to understand that even if I really do think I'm a "slut" this doesn't mean I'm no longer a human. I expect men who believe I've had a lot of sex to know that no means no, no matter who says it. Again, these expectations have proven so far reasonable with the majority of men, and I expect that men who resist them have it in them to not be assholes.

I have one more expectation. I expect that when a man flouts the rules of morality and decency and harasses or assaults a woman, we treat him like the raving douchebag he is, and bring criminal charges where applicable.

Reading back over my list of expectations—demands—the part of me still socialized in traditional femininity flinches. A woman running down a list of expectations calls to mind unpleasant stereotypes: a bridezilla stomping her foot at a florist who used the word *can't*, Meryl Streep in a power suit barking orders at a hapless assistant, a grim-faced church lady denouncing the evils of fornication. But really, this list of expectations isn't so outrageous. The ability to live in the world, have fun, be flirtatious, make jokes, dress alluringly, have sex, and do all these things while still expecting the law to protect you from violent assault? These sorts of things should be expectations. Men—at least privileged white men who aren't continually targeted by the police—experience lives where these expectations don't even need to be articulated, but are simply part of the air they breathe. All SlutWalk is asking is that the same opportunities be offered to women.

Criminalizing Circumcision:
Self-Hatred as Public Policy
Marty Klein

Full disclosure: I'm circumcised.

Too much information? Tell that to the people—well-meaning or otherwise—who have actually created a ballot measure to criminalize circumcision in San Francisco.[1] Yes, in November 2011, San Franciscans vote on whether or not babies (and all minors) can be circumcised. In the wake of the ban's (unlikely) passage, one can imagine the surgical equivalent of speakeasies or underground abortion clinics to which families bring little Joshua, Omar, or Justin.

The bill has been driven primarily by the psychological anguish of a small number of activists. The main source of information about their emotional torment is contained in the bill's language: *It is unlawful to circumcise, excise, cut, or mutilate the whole or any part of the foreskin, testicles, or penis of another person who has not attained the age of 18 years.*

Equating the removal of an infant's foreskin with the "mutilation" of the testicles or penis is ignorance, willful distortion, or delusion. No one in the city has been accused of touching any minor's testicles or penis (Catholic priests notwithstanding). But lumping these together with the routine, nearly painless removal of foreskin—which has no impact on later physical function—shows just how theatrical the bill's sponsors are. They are acting out their own odd sense of bereavement with a grand display of concern for future generations.

As a sex therapist for 31 years, I have talked with more men about their penises than an office full of urologists. We've discussed concerns about size, shape, color, and the angle of the dangle. We've talked about the ability to give and receive pleasure. We've talked about the amount, color, taste, smell, and consistency of semen. We've talked about what women (and other men) supposedly like about penises. And some men have talked about how they feel about being circumcised or not circumcised. If I ask, almost all men are fine as they are; if a man brings it up first, he's almost always convinced he'd be better off different than he is—the cut guys want to be uncut, and the uncut guys want to be cut.

Most patients who wish they were different are perfectly sane people who are somewhat overconcerned about their penises. Others are a bit less sane. And a few are intensely involved with their feelings to the point of ignoring science, logic, and the sworn statements of one or more lovers.

I believe the people behind the San Francisco proposal to ban circumcision are among the latter group. In 31 years of talking with men about their penises, I have never met a man who felt damaged, mutilated, or emasculated by his circumcision who did not have other emotional problems as well. The pain they claim to remember from the brief procedure is impossible; the rejection from "all women" a childish overgeneralization; the sense of being incomplete a neurotic problem that has other sources.

Yes, there are a few sensible reasons that some sincere people want to discourage routine circumcision. But this is dramatically different from men who feel mutilated or disgusted with their penis blaming all their life's problems on an event they can't possibly remember.

The sexual effects of circumcision are clear: there are none. Say what you want about foreskins protecting penile sensitivity—virtually no one complains that their penis isn't sensitive enough. I make my living listening to stories of sexual frustration and dissatisfaction, and they almost never center on "my penis doesn't feel things intensely enough." When they do, it almost invariably involves a serious emotional problem (guilt, Asperger's syndrome, anxiety, trauma, dissociation, etc.), and the guy is as likely to be uncircumcised as not.

The idea that a penis being 2 percent or 20 percent more sensitive (from the protective action of a foreskin) would prevent men's sexual distress is nonsense. You might as well say that bigger testicles would make sex better. The truth is, most men (like most women) do very few of the things that could enhance their enjoyment of sex: relaxation or meditation beforehand; more kissing; communicating more about likes and dislikes; experimenting more with nonerogenous parts of both bodies; taking more time; starting when they're not already tired; covering contraception more reliably; using a lubricant before it's "necessary"; and learning to enjoy sex with a bit of light in the room.

Men who cry that they can't enjoy sex without a foreskin are in real pain—but it isn't really about their circumcision.

The United Nations recognizes the health benefits of circumcision; the World Health Organization is now promoting a huge circumcision campaign in sub-Saharan Africa, which has been wildly successful in reducing HIV infections in Uganda, Kenya, and South Africa. Ironically, it's world-famous San Francisco urologist Ira Sharlip who's been asked to advise the project. Halfway around the world, the Philippines recently offered free circumcisions for poor people, who lined up enthusiastically.

Indeed, studies around the world show that circumcision reduces urinary and other infections, has no negative sexual effects, and is rarely dangerous when performed according to simple public health guidelines. There is absolutely no evidence that the sexual experiences of circumcised and uncircumcised men are different for them or their partners (outside of their partners' simple personal taste, of course). What do women prefer? Most prefer the penises they've spent their lives with.

As a therapist, I am sworn to empathize with the pain of every man, woman, and child in my office. I am also devoted to reducing suffering by helping people understand the meaning behind their pain, the better to resolve and escape from it.

As a citizen, my sworn concern is to keep emotion out of public policy, the better to foster the impartiality of science and enhance everyone's well-being. So I urge anyone who feels damaged by their circumcision to get as much therapy as necessary, as much good sex as possible—and to keep their self-admittedly damaged psyches away from public policy. Guys, pleasure and intimacy await—as soon as you make friends with your penis. The ballot box is not the place to work out your self-loathing.

On July 28, 2011, California Superior Court Judge Loretta Giorgi ordered the proposed ban on circumcision removed from the upcoming San Francisco ballot. She explained that medical procedures, just like marriage and driver's licenses, can only be regulated by the state, not by individual municipalities.

Proponents of the ban vowed to take their drive to the state level.

In the wake of my posting of this piece, I received over 100 responses, comments, and emails. Although a few were supportive, the overwhelming majority were negative. Some cited the various international associations that don't support circumcision. Others cited statistics purporting to show that circumcision is dangerous—the extremely rare infection and even the one-in-a-million death.

But most responses dispensed with such civilized conventions as citations and statistics, however bogus or agenda-driven. These correspondents were generally anguished, enraged, or both. They questioned my credentials as a sexologist and as a psychotherapist, often in very nasty terms. They powerfully described their sadness, hopelessness, and bitterness. They felt mutilated and abused, and betrayed by what they interpreted as my dismissal of their pain.

As I said, that pain is real, but it goes much deeper than circumcision. These men feel alienated from masculinity, from sexuality, from their bodies. Unfortunately, this is not rare in America. As people who struggle with anorexia, obesity, addiction, violent impulses, and lack of sexual desire show us, you don't have to be circumcised to feel that alienation.

Some substantive issues did recur in the dozens of negative responses I received. Let me address them directly:

Why is male circumcision acceptable to those who reject female genital cutting?

Because the latter brutally damages an entire system of a woman's body, reduces sexual function for a lifetime (not just sexual pleasure, but sexual function—that's the intention), and often leads to lifelong infections. Virtually all male circumcision is free of subsequent infection, sexual dysfunction, or urinary damage.

Circumcision is done before a male can consent, so why not just prevent it until adulthood?

Our society accepts that parents are responsible for making virtually all decisions for their babies. Parents choose a wide range of medical practices for them without waiting for them to reach adulthood—for example, vaccination, ear piercing, invasive testing, many elective and corrective surgeries.

A circumcised man can't know the sexual pleasure he's missing, so he shouldn't insist that the procedure is harmless for his (or other) babies.

This is a curious (and common) argument. If a man can't know what he's missing, how can he miss it—as so many anticircumcision activists claim? Most men could immediately increase their sexual pleasure by drinking less, kissing more, quitting smoking, talking to their partners, and starting sex earlier in the evening when they're more energetic. The common unwillingness to take these steps trivializes any demand for "more pleasure."

I am certainly no apologist for circumcision. As we say about abortion, nude beaches, and nonmonogamy, if you don't believe in it, don't do it.

But legislating sexuality is the way citizens most often demand that society deal with their personal demons. Fear of our kids being molested? Create horrible sex offender laws. Fear of teens being sexual? Criminalize teen sexuality and "sexting." Fear of our neighbors being too kinky? Shut down swingers' clubs. Fear of our kids actually learning something about sex? Destroy sex education and sanitize libraries and network TV.

When emotion drives public policy, everyone suffers. The pain of stifled sexual expression and the obsessive promotion of sexual fear, guilt, and shame are ultimately far more destructive than any distress about circumcision could possibly be.

Endnotes

1 In California, a group of people can get a proposition on the general election ballot by collecting sufficient signatures on a petition. Signature collecting is now a huge business in the state; out-of-state money often drives the process.

The Worship of Female Pleasure
Tracy Clark-Flory

Nicole Daedone pulls her long dirty-blond locks into a bun, rolls up the sleeves of her crisp white dress shirt, and readies her lube. On the table in front of her there is a woman, naked only from the waist down, with her knees spread wide. The 40-something founder of OneTaste, a center dedicated to "mindful sexuality," is about to give a live and impromptu demonstration of orgasmic meditation ("OMing" for short) in a conference room at the sophisticated Le Méridien hotel in San Francisco. She takes a long look between the volunteer's legs and enthuses to the audience of roughly 40 women: "Oh my god, it's beautiful. It's an electric rose color. The swelling is already beginning."

Before long, Daedone is hunched over and vigorously stroking the woman's most sensitive "spot"—the "upper left quadrant" of the clitoris—with just her forefinger. The recipient moans wildly as though she is being taken over by a spirit and Daedone urges her on: "Good girl. Good, good. Reach, reach, reach, reach." As the woman's groans peak, Daedone lets out a throaty exhalation that sounds as if it belongs in a Lamaze class. Two audience members overcome by the intensity of the performance are silently crying. The demonstration, which is part of a weekend-long women's retreat, continues for 15 minutes.

It is both arousing and deeply bizarre.

It isn't every weekend that I find myself watching a woman being repeatedly brought to orgasm in front of a live audience—but I hardly expected normality when I asked to sit in on the workshop. Instead, I was hoping to get a candid view of Daedone ahead of the release of her book, *Slow Sex: The Art and Craft of the Female Orgasm*, which attempts to market her meditative practice to a broader audience. That is a challenging task when your practice involves a bunch of clothed men (and sometimes women) gathering in a room and manually stimulating half-naked female "research partners" for exactly 15 minutes. Two years ago, a *New York Times* feature detailed the eyebrow-raising practices at One-Taste's "urban retreat center" in the wacky-woo Bay Area and described Daedone as "a polarizing personality, whom admirers venerate as a sex diva, although some former members say she has cultlike powers over her followers." Since that high-profile coverage, OneTaste has become a bit more circumspect, but clearly not so much as to bar spontaneous OMing demonstrations—at an event initially advertised as including no "sexual activity." (But, you see, Daedone has a tendency to go off script—that, or else appearing to do so is part of her script; it's hard to say.)

Dig beneath the freaky OMing exterior and the core of her message is very marketable to the mainstream. Consider the demand for "female Viagra," a product estimated to have a $2 billion market. Study after study tells us that women desperately want more sexual desire and more orgasms (or orgasms, period). Female desire and pleasure are what Daedone is all about—to the point that many criticize her for being too womancentric. (After I explained the OneTaste mission to a male friend, he exclaimed incredulously: "The man never gets a turn? That's messed up!")

Just as with the slow food movement, the idea behind "slow sex" is to slow down enough to know when you're hungry or satiated, to identify your cravings, to savor every sensation, and to be present in this very moment. As she writes in the book, the aim is to give women the "permission to enjoy the journey, rather than pushing them ever sooner to the finale." With that comes a recasting of what orgasm means: "We have been defining the term 'orgasm' as the traditional definition of male orgasm: climax," she writes. "Climax is often a part of orgasm, but it is not the sum total. Make this distinction, and you change the whole game." (I met a woman at the workshop who says she had OMed 300 or so times and only climaxed once.)

These basic ideas are not especially controversial; they are pretty intuitive as well as having roots in the practice of Tantric sex. More generally, her emphasis on mindfulness—a sexual take on "Be here now"—borrows heavily from Eastern philosophies. Daedone's background in gender studies also shows: she speaks passionately about negative cultural conditioning around sex and all the ways that women are taught to replace their own desires with men's. Balancing the academic side of OneTaste is the fashionable, cosmopolitan vibe of Daedone and her inner circle, a crew of supremely attractive, sensual, and pristinely dressed women in their 30s and 40s. Think *Sex and the City*'s Samantha at a Buddhist retreat. Daedone can just as readily sound like a New Age sex guru as she can an everywoman ranting to her girlfriends about frustrations in the bedroom. There is an Oprahesque strain of feminism here, too: In her manifesto, she reveres the sort of woman whose epitaph would read, "She scaled mountains, in hiking boots and in heels." Where there's an Oprah comparison, there is good old-fashioned capitalism: there are products for sale on the group's website, including OneTaste-branded lube, special OMing pillows and an instructional DVD on the practice. There's also a "slow sex" coaching program that costs anywhere from $4,000 to $11,000. The weekend retreat I attended was $495.

In between Daedone's workshop lectures, the motley group of women, ranging in age from their early 20s to their 60s, engaged in a series of intimacy exercises. We were encouraged to enter a makeshift photo booth to have our personal "pussy portrait" taken, and then printouts of the shots were displayed for all to see. At one point we were instructed to gather in the center of the room, standing close enough to one another that we could "feel each other's body heat," and whisper to one another previously unspoken desires; some of these secrets were written on Post-its (the messages ranged from "rape fantasy" to "soft kisses") and pasted on the walls of the conference room.

It's easy to see why some call her a cult leader: When she shines her light on you, you feel special and seen. Before the OMing demonstration, she told the room: "There's all these questions as OneTaste gets bigger about fucking appropriateness… And there's a reporter in the room," she said, gesturing toward me. Daedone narrowed her eyes and continued: "But, quite frankly, as a human being I think you're one of us witchy women"—then she winked at me, and my insides melted. That's the thing about Daedone: she can disarm you with the bat of her lashes—or a flick of her index finger. She's an extremely compelling and charismatic character, and all the more so because there is actual substance and intellect behind the sexpert shtick.

Ultimately, she elevates the female orgasm to a level of religious and spiritual practice. "Slow sex" is at first relatable and approachable but quickly turns woo-woo and New Age. Daedone's philosophy is a refreshing counterpoint to the porny mainstream, but it's certainly hard to picture Middle America embracing orgasmic meditation. Not even most coast-dwelling liberals are ready to be intimately stroked in a roomful of strangers.

Sex, Lies, and Hush Money
Katherine Spillar

This is the story of an illicit sexual relationship between a powerful US senator and his female campaign treasurer, and of the equally powerful male political figures who allegedly helped cover it up. It's a story where so-called family values and religiosity meet abuse of power. And it's the story of a handful of no-nonsense women watchdogs who have been trying to bring the culprits to justice.

The man at the center of this story is now former US Senator John Ensign (R-Nev.), who earned a 100 percent approval rating from the "pro-family" Christian Coalition. He stepped down from Congress on May 3, 2011, just a day before he was to give a deposition under oath to the Senate Ethics Committee—which had spent nearly two years investigating his actions. On May 10, the committee issued its stunning report, detailing "substantial credible evidence" that Ensign had violated federal criminal and civil laws, including lying to federal investigators about illegal payments to the woman and her husband.

Still seated in Congress is another major player in the saga, Senator Tom Coburn (R–Okla.)—another powerful conservative Republican, who has advocated the death penalty for abortion providers. Coburn, whose name is throughout the report, may have played a central role in trying to negotiate a settlement with the woman's husband (also an employee of Ensign's)—though Coburn has denied this. And playing a minor but still telling role in the report is the former Pennsylvania Republican senator and staunch social conservative Rick Santorum, who alerted Ensign to the fact that the whole sordid tale was about to be leaked to the media.

The cast of heroic women in this case is led by Melanie Sloan, executive director of the DC congressional watchdog group CREW (Citizens for Responsibility and Ethics in Washington). It filed ethics complaints against both Ensign and Coburn, alleging that the latter helped cover up the affair. Carol Elder Bruce, a well-regarded DC attorney hired as special counsel to the Senate Ethics Committee, authored the report that excoriated Ensign. And, finally, Senator Barbara Boxer (D–Calif.)—chair of the Ethics Committee—ultimately won a unanimous bipartisan vote to refer the committee's findings to the attorney general for possible criminal prosecution.

But significant questions remain. Why hasn't the Justice Department prosecuted Ensign? Why hasn't the Ethics Committee now turned its attention to Coburn's role? In other words, why haven't those men who so doggedly stand up for "family values" been brought to account for their not just hypocritical but possibly illegal behavior?

Special Counsel Bruce's report to the Ethics Committee reads a bit like a cheap novel. In it, we learn that the woman Senator Ensign had a sexual liaison with, Cynthia Hampton, worked for him as treasurer of his campaign committee and PAC. Her husband, Doug, was Ensign's top administrative assistant in his Senate office—really, his co-chief of staff.

But the Hamptons had been more than just employees. Cynthia was Ensign's wife Darlene's friend from high school, and the two men met while dating their future wives. At the Ensign wedding, Cynthia was a bridesmaid.

The Ensigns helped the Hamptons move from California to their Nevada neighborhood, providing tens of thousands of dollars to refinance an expensive house the Hamptons couldn't quite afford. In addition, Ensign helped get both of them jobs in Nevada. The two couples sent their children to the same private school—with the Ensigns again assisting with tens of thousands of dollars in support. The families took vacations together, spent most Sundays together, and Doug and John played golf together several times a week.

Then, at some point in late 2007, Ensign began pursuing a sexual affair with Cynthia. This was certainly in opposition to the morality he espoused to the public, such as his 1998 call for President Bill Clinton's resignation after a sexual liaison with Monica Lewinsky, or his statement that "marriage is the cornerstone on which our society was founded," delivered on the Senate floor in favor of the antigay Federal Marriage Amendment in 2004.

Moreover, it's unlikely that this affair was truly consensual. Senator Ensign "just [wouldn't] stop" and "kept calling and calling" and "would never take no for an answer," explained Cynthia Hampton, according to the Ethics Committee report. Eventually she gave in.

"She was really worried about her family" is how Melanie

Sloan describes Hampton's motivation. "And by the same token … she and her husband relied on this guy [Ensign] for their incomes, and he paid for their kids' school. She was worried about angering him. She would've ended it but he kept pushing so much." Indeed, the Senate ethics report found substantial credible evidence that Ensign's behavior constituted sexual harassment. It emphasized that Ensign had "enormous power" over Hampton and her husband, as they were both employed by him, and he ultimately forced them to leave his office because of the sexual relationship.

Doug Hampton found out about the liaison just a few weeks after it began and confronted Ensign (reportedly chasing him around an airport parking lot), and the senator and Ms. Hampton agreed the next day to end it. But on a trip with his boss to Iraq and Afghanistan in February 2008, Hampton discovered that it was continuing. Not knowing what else to do, he reached out to a man he thought Ensign might listen to: Tim Coe.

Coe is the son of Doug Coe, the powerful head of "the Family" (also known as the Fellowship Foundation), a secretive, mostly male, right-wing Christian fundamentalist group. Tim Coe recommended bringing Senator Coburn into the discussion, describing him as a "higher authority, someone much bigger than me." When they were in Washington, Ensign and Coburn, both Family members, resided with other members of Congress at the group's infamous 12-bedroom C Street row house.

Operating under the tax-deductible status of a religious organization, the Family, founded in 1935, cultivates and networks powerful key men in business, government, and the military, in the US and worldwide. It is best known for its one major public event, the annual nonpartisan National Prayer Breakfast. But as Jeff Sharlet pointed out in his 2008 book, *The Family*, it wields tremendous behind-the-scenes influence, sometimes in support of despotic leaders in places such as Uganda and Somalia.

And despite the religious mission of the Family, three of the most salacious political sex scandals in recent years have involved men who lived or prayed at C Street: Ensign, former South Carolina Republican governor Mark Sanford (of Appalachian Trail fame) and former representative Chip Pickering (R-Miss.), another ardent defender of "traditional marriage" who's said to have conducted his out-of-wedlock liaison while residing at the C Street house.

"The Family doesn't really care about political corruption," says Sharlet, who lived undercover at a Family-owned house and met Ensign on a visit to C Street. "They think it's wrong but they don't care about it. So when Ensign starts messing around … it's about preserving power."

According to the Ethics Committee report, both Coburn and Coe essentially took charge of ending the affair. Coburn helped convene a Valentine's Day meeting between the senator and Doug Hampton at C Street, where Ensign reportedly wept and vowed to repent. When Hampton began to become physically threatening, Coburn asked him to leave, saying, "We'll take it from here. We'll take care of this." Two days later, Hampton saw Ensign's car in a hotel parking lot and called Tim Coe again. Coe called the senator and told him, "I know exactly where you are. I know exactly what you are doing. Put your pants on and go home."

As the cheap-romance plot thickened, Doug Hampton confronted Ensign again the next day. But this time, instead of being contrite, the senator told Hampton that he wanted to marry Cynthia and that Doug couldn't work for him anymore. He would tell Cynthia that he wanted Doug out so that he could meet with her more easily—without his aide's knowledge of his schedule. The affair continued sporadically for months.

By forcing out Doug Hampton—and soon after that Cynthia—Senator Ensign would be leaving the Hamptons with no jobs and a large mortgage. That's when talk of "transition finances" and a plan to get the Hamptons to move out of Nevada was formulated. According to the Ethics Committee report, Tim Coe, who spearheaded the plan, said he considered Senator Coburn part of the team to work out the "financial piece," and that Coburn was supportive of the overall transition plan. Moreover, Coe explained that Doug Hampton thought Coburn could "deliver" Senator Ensign's father, the wealthy casino mogul Michael Ensign.

Tim Coe told the committee that Coburn called the senior Ensign at his request. Whether or not this call happened is a matter of dispute: Coe insists that Coburn made it; Coburn denies it. Under questioning by the committee's special counsel, Michael Ensign "allowed as how the call may have taken place." While on its face this he-said/he-said seems unimportant, in political scandals it's the cover-up that gets politicians into the most legal trouble.

In Sloan's view, "It's clear that Coburn lied, even in talking to Senate investigators—he told them he hadn't talked to Michael Ensign. But Tim Coe remembers specifically that [Coburn] called Michael." Sloan adds, "Lying to Senate investigators would be a crime."

Meanwhile, Senator Ensign was working on his own transition plan for Doug Hampton, getting married political operatives Lindsey and Mike Slanker to let Hampton use their Nevada political consulting firm, November Inc., as a base for obtaining lobbying clients. The committee report detailed how Ensign made "extraordinary" attempts to set up various jobs for Hampton—even instructing his chief of staff to bully one constituent into hiring the man with the threat of cutting off access to Ensign.

Federal law, however, prohibits Senate employees from lobbying the Senate for a year after they leave their employment. Not only did it appear Hampton started lobbying immediately after he officially left Ensign's office in May 2008, but the committee found substantial credible evidence that Ensign helped Hampton violate the post-employment contact ban at least 30 times.

In addition, Hampton—by his own notes—engaged with Senator Ensign in a series of negotiations in early April about a severance payment. On April 7, the Hamptons received a check made out to them and two of their children for $96,000 from the Ensign Family Trust—an account controlled by the senator's parents, Michael and Sharon.

Senator Ensign and the senior Ensigns gave affidavits to federal investigators stating that the payment was simply a gift and that the senator hadn't requested it. Under questioning by the special counsel, however, Michael and Sharon acknowledged they did not carefully review the affidavits before signing them, leading the committee to conclude that it was actually a severance payment. If it was, that is a violation of a federal law against private donations for Senate office expenses and constitutes an unlawful and unreported campaign contribution. Further, the committee found substantial and credible evidence that Ensign had made false statements regarding the payments.

But there's more. A year after receiving the $96,000, Hampton hired Las Vegas attorney Dan Albregts to help secure an additional financial settlement from Ensign. Here again, the committee report states, Senator Coburn got involved.

In May 2009, Coburn began to negotiate with Albregts,

looking to come up with an amount that Ensign could pay to make the Hamptons move out of Nevada. According to Albregts, he and Coburn eventually agreed on $2.8 million—a figure that Ensign rejected. In his testimony to the committee, Coburn denies being a "negotiator," saying he was just passing information.

This is where ex-senator and then Fox News commentator Rick Santorum enters the picture. Asking for Santorum's help, Hampton forwarded the former senator an email he'd written to Fox News, in which he laid out the issues and pleaded for a meeting. Instead, Santorum forwarded the personal communication to Ensign, effectively alerting him to the fact that Hampton was about to go public.

Ensign immediately called an emergency late-night meeting with his staff, telling them about the brewing situation and strategizing about how to deal with it. The next morning he held a press conference to publicly apologize for the affair. Three days later, his spokesperson would accuse Doug Hampton of blackmail and extortion in making "exorbitant demands for cash and other financial benefits."

CREW stepped into the midst of the messy case after reports of the $96,000 "gift" were leaked. The watchdog group, which *Ms.* magazine wrote about when CREW was taking on alleged corruption by House Majority Leader Tom DeLay, filed its complaint with the Ethics Committee in June 2009. CREW alleged Senator Ensign had discriminated "on the basis of sex in the form of sexual harassment" and alerted the committee to the possible illegal payment.

At the same time, CREW filed a companion complaint with the Federal Election Commission (FEC), asserting that the $96,000 payment was an illegal campaign contribution. In March 2010, the FEC's general counsel urged the commission to inves-

tigate the matter, but in November of that year the recommenda-
tion was rejected.

Nonetheless, the Ethics Committee, chaired by Senator Boxer,
took CREW's complaint seriously and opened an investigation.
Two years later, the damning report it released stated that, had
Ensign not resigned, the special counsel was confident that the
evidence would have warranted Ensign's possible expulsion from
Congress. He would have been the first senator since 1862 to be
so disgraced.

The committee found substantial credible evidence that Ensign conspired to violate (and aided and abetted violations of)
federal lobbying law, made false statements to cover up severance
payments to the Hamptons, obstructed the Ethics Committee's
investigation, and sexually harassed an employee. The report
also found that Ensign violated his own Senate office policies,
including those regarding sexual harassment. Since that would
have been cause for termination of one of his employees, the rules
should have been applied to Ensign as well. In other words, he
should have fired himself.

The fact that the committee's report characterized Ensign's
violation of his office policies as discrimination and sexual harassment is a significant outcome of the investigation. In effect,
says Melanie Sloan, the report elevates the importance of sexual
harassment as a violation of Senate rules.

"I think what is striking about this is the levels that people
went to to help Ensign cover up this affair," says Debra Katz,
a Washington DC lawyer who specializes in sexual harassment
cases. "If this were a civil case, these clowns would be legally
responsible for aiding and abetting the type of sexual harassment
that took place."

So Ensign is gone from the Senate. Now what?

As of this writing, the Department of Justice has not indicated whether it will act on the Ethics Committee's referral that it investigate and consider criminally prosecuting the former senator. It had halted its investigation in December 2010, but now a wealth of new evidence is available, thanks to the committee's investigation.

Also, the Federal Election Commission has not indicated whether it will consider reopening its investigation of Senator Ensign, as the Ethics Committee has urged. Finally, the Ethics Committee itself has not yet acted on CREW's separate October 2009 complaint to investigate Senator Tom Coburn for his role in allegedly covering up Ensign's affair and for perhaps knowingly allowing Doug Hampton to lobby him in violation of the one-year post-employment ban. "It's incumbent on the committee to do something," says Sloan. "By the way, none of the other senators have said anything about Coburn's behavior either, including the Democrats. It's the clubby Senate."

Asked about his role in the matter in July 2009, when the story first broke in the national media, Coburn said he only counseled Ensign as a doctor and as a deacon, and he considered that counsel a "privileged communication that I will never reveal to anybody." It should be said here that Senator Coburn is indeed a doctor: a family practitioner specializing in obstetrics and allergies.

As for Coburn's role as a deacon, Sloan has this to say: "First of all, a deacon doesn't have legal confidentiality, and second, Ensign wasn't in his church." And, she points out, "Presumably Ensign didn't need medical advice, so he wasn't a patient."

Coburn has emphatically challenged the Ethics Committee report's portrait of his role in negotiating compensation for Hampton. "That's a totally inaccurate characterization of what happened," he told C–SPAN recently. "The story you hear is not an accurate reflection of what happened." He said he feels good about what he did, and that he would do it again in the same way if given the chance. "We put two families back together with multiple children—both marriages are stable right now," he says.

Hardly. Doug and Cynthia Hampton are in the process of getting divorced. Cynthia has filed for bankruptcy.

Meanwhile, the only person facing criminal prosecution by the Department of Justice so far is Doug Hampton. In March, he was indicted on seven counts stemming from the lobbying activity he undertook after Ensign fired him. "Why have laws that only apply to the less powerful?" asks Melanie Sloan. "The Department of Justice ought to be trying really hard to prosecute Ensign. The only people who are suffering in this story are the ones who blew the whistle. There's an incredible unfairness here."

The Dynamics of Sexual Acceleration
Chris Sweeney

Susan and Brendan had been dating for a month when they decided to spend a weekend together in New York. They had met in
Falls Church, Virginia, and while Susan was not completely sold
on Brendan, sneaking around the office and having a quickie in
the copy room kept her interested. As they unpacked their bags
and settled into a dingy hotel on the Lower East Side, the tension
that had mounted during their five-hour drive snapped.

The couple dived into bed with the eagerness that accom-
panies a new relationship. But the much-anticipated session pe-
tered out in two minutes, before Susan could even warm up.
"What the fuck is wrong with you?" she asked as Brendan rolled
off her. This marked at least the fifth time in their relationship that Brendan had ejaculated too quickly for Susan's liking,
and despite the fact that he always reciprocated "with a good
munch," her patience had peaked. Brendan retreated downstairs

for a cigarette, wishing to avoid further interrogation.

Is there something wrong with Brendan? It depends on whom you ask. The prospect of a sex-filled vacation may have put him in a state of anxiety that was manifested in this sexual shortcoming. Or Brendan may be genetically predisposed to having a low ejaculatory threshold, possessing a hypersensitive penis that lets him last only a few minutes. It may be that the cascade of dopamine, serotonin, oxytocin, and other neurochemicals is at fault. Some would suggest Brendan's early ejaculation could be linked to how he masturbates or is embedded in his pubescent sexual encounters. Or, of course, there is always the possibility that nothing is wrong with Brendan, that Susan's expectations just don't align with his capabilities for impromptu intercourse.

Susan's postcopulatory inquiry into what the fuck was wrong took Brendan down a notch, and their tryst fizzled out soon after. Men with rapid ejaculation worry that their partners will leave them, and the added anxiety just makes the condition worse.

The length of time to orgasm is highly variable in men. A 2005 study published in *The Journal of Sexual Medicine* used stopwatches to measure intravaginal ejaculation latency, or how long a man lasts from the start of intercourse until ejaculation. The study looked at 5,600 couples from the United States, the United Kingdom, Turkey, Spain, and the Netherlands, and revealed a median time of 5.4 minutes, and a range from under a minute to about 45 minutes. The average time varied for each country, with the Turks coming first at 3.7 minutes. Condoms had no impact on the average time, and being circumcised yielded an insignificant benefit. Another study, also published in 2005 in *The Journal of Sexual Medicine*, revealed a median time of 7.5 minutes among 1,380 American men not considered to have ejaculation difficulties. The study also included 207 men considered to be premature ejaculators, who clocked an average of 1.8 minutes.

Premature ejaculation is a term everyone has heard but few can define beyond the obvious "when a guy comes too early." A taboo looms over the issue, with most conversations relegated to punch lines or dense medical literature. To be fair, before there was ED there was impotence, and that wasn't a choice talking point either.

Determining what constitutes premature ejaculation has recently been the occasion of increasing debate. Is it the inability to last more than a predetermined time? Is it not being able to recognize when ejaculation will occur?

The focus on creating a universal definition of primary premature ejaculation is driven in part by the pharmaceutical industry's interest in selling drugs that make a man last longer. Johnson & Johnson's drug for early ejaculation, dapoxetine, is approved in a handful of overseas markets under the brand name Priligy. The drug, rejected by the FDA in 2005, has been shown to lead to a threefold increase in duration when taken in a 60-milligram dose about an hour before sex. Dapoxetine is a selective serotonin reuptake inhibitor, as are the antidepressants Prozac and Paxil. A well-known side effect of most SSRIs is delayed ejaculation, leading many doctors to prescribe them to men in need of a few extra thrusts. Using a side effect of a drug to treat a condition for which the drug is not approved is hardly ideal, but no FDA-approved treatment exists.

Shionogi is a Japanese pharmaceutical company based in Osaka. It recently wrapped up Phase III studies—the last and largest stage of testing, when a drug is compared with other treatments—on an experimental compound dubbed PSD502. The drug is a combination of the topical anesthetics lidocaine and prilocaine and is sprayed on the head of the penis a few minutes before sex. In studies of about 1,000 men and their female partners, PSD502 prolonged the point of no return from an average of 0.6 minutes to 3.5 minutes. There is nothing novel about using drugs to desensitize the nether regions, but most such drugs are creams, and rubbing cream on the penis of a man who is trying to last longer is ill-advised. Dr. Donald Manning, Shionogi's chief medical officer, says the spray appears to reduce sensation without numbing the penis—always a good thing if you actually want to enjoy sex—and claims that fewer than two percent of men who used it reported numbness.

Redefining Premature Ejaculation

The pharmaceutical industry's interest in serving a vast market of premature ejaculators isn't the only factor behind arguments about how the condition should be defined. *The Diagnostic and Statistical Manual of Mental Disorders*, the American Psychiatric Association's reference text, is being revised for the publication of its fifth edition in 2013. Some people have criticized the *DSM*'s current definition of premature ejaculation as being too subjective. The symptoms of PE, according to the fourth edition of the *DSM*, include "ejaculation with minimal sexual stimulation before, on or shortly after penetration and before the person wishes it."

Dr. Robert Taylor Segraves, professor of psychiatry at Case Western Reserve University and a member of the *DSM* revision panel, says this definition is so vague any number of people can be diagnosed with the problem. Some studies even classify men who last well beyond five minutes as premature ejaculators. "It sounds kind of meaningless at that point," Segraves says. "We need greater precision."

The draft proposal of the new edition of the *DSM* recommends dropping *premature* and renaming the condition *early ejaculation.* Segraves and Michael Perelman, a Manhattan-based psychologist who is president of the Society for Sex Therapy and Research, agree that *premature* has a pejorative connotation. However, Perelman—who also serves as a consultant for pharmaceutical companies—predicts that in the future it will likely be known as PE, just as erectile dysfunction is now called ED.

A few years back, Plethora Solutions, a UK-based drug firm, awarded an unrestricted grant to the International Society for Sexual Medicine to explore the evidence. A crew of 21 leaders ranging in specialties from psychiatry to neurourology met in Amsterdam in 2007 to prepare a diagnostic blueprint for men who ejaculate too quickly. After looking at the data, the leaders emerged with what is now considered to be the gold-standard definition. The ISSM's definition regards the dysfunction as "ejaculation which always or nearly always occurs prior to or within about one minute of vaginal penetration," rather than simply before a person wishes it to occur.

The ISSM, like the DSM, takes into account the strain that PE can place on a man, his partner, and their relationship. But it is the one-minute benchmark—the quantitative end point—that may prove vital in bringing PE drugs to our prescription-hungry nation.

Plethora Solutions's decision to give the ISSM a grant for a definition was not just a gesture of goodwill. Plethora developed the above-mentioned ejaculation-delaying spray, PSD502, and licensed it to Sciele Pharma, which was later acquired by Shionogi. Should Shionogi succeed in becoming the first company to have an FDA-approved drug for premature ejaculation, Plethora could see a windfall in royalties. Manning, Shionogi's chief medical officer, says the company used the one-minute benchmark in the data it collected, as well as aspects of control and distress. In fact, data from the study show that men who were given the drug ranked significantly higher on a scale of ejaculatory control than men given a placebo.

Shionogi and J&J—which is analyzing its own dapoxetine data for a potential FDA resubmission—aren't the only drug makers who hope to crack this market. Sarah Terry, president of biomedical data provider Life Science Analytics, says about 20 players are looking to get in. GlaxoSmithKline is among them, with two drugs in development: one designed to inhibit oxytocin and the other an SSRI. Both are in Phase II testing, when scientists determine if a proposed medication is actually associated with a therapeutic benefit.

Patent Gold Mine
Premature ejaculation is attractive to drug companies because it represents an entirely new market at a time when they need to replenish their pipelines with new compounds. Big Pharma is hurtling toward a patent cliff, and generic companies are ready to pounce on the opportunity to churn out cheaper versions of Lipitor and Viagra, which come off patent in 2011 and 2012. Terry says that between 2008 and 2014, $113 billion worth of drugs will have their patents expire.

The potential of a drug for premature ejaculation dwarfs that of an erectile dysfunction drug. Estimates vary—mainly because of the definition issue and trouble in designing studies—but between 20 and 30 percent of the population could be considered premature ejaculators. One market study, from Datamonitor, estimates that in 2010 the US population of early ejaculators between the ages of 20 and 59 was 25.8 million, compared with 9.5 million men in need of bonder drugs. "I think the FDA is ultimately willing to approve a drug for premature ejaculation," Terry says. "The challenge at this stage is just defining what that actually means."

Research Pioneers
In the days of King Charles II, the last Spanish Hapsburg ruler and one of the most regal premature ejaculators on record, sexual dysfunctions were the product of witchcraft. Innovative treatments included exorcisms and urinating through your wedding ring or through the keyhole of the church where you were married. Fast forward to the early 20th century and you'll come across a sea of erotic snake oil, including an arsenic-containing elixir in Dr. Frank Miller's 1913 tome, *Domestic Medical Practice*. In the wake of Kinsey in the late 1950s came the work of William Masters and Virginia Johnson, better known as Masters and Johnson. The duo developed the still popular squeeze technique to prolong sex, which, as its name implies, involves putting a stranglehold on the head of the penis before ejaculation. Studies have demonstrated its efficacy, but evidence suggests that without regular reapplication the positive effects wear off. Also, it can be awkward to ask someone you're sleeping with for the first time to put your dick in a death grip.

"Masters couldn't do any analysis—he didn't have any funding—so what he did was hire prostitutes and observe them, interview them, identify how they had sex and what the sexual issues of their lives were," says Dr. Irwin Goldstein, director of sexual medicine at Alvarado Hospital in San Diego. Goldstein, who was an acquaintance of Masters's, notes that the atmosphere surrounding sexual research was so restrictive in the early days of his work that Masters struggled to get medical texts about female reproductive anatomy. "The thing is, prostitutes saw a lot of men who were anxious and stressed, so his formulations were made on bad observations because of a biased population. It was their theory, which is perpetuated even in 2010, that 90-plus percent of all sexual problems are due to psychological issues: anxiety, humiliation, fear, depression."

Goldstein is editor in chief of the *Journal of Sexual Medicine* and also a drug company consultant. For more than 20 years he was funded by the National Institutes of Health to study sexual function and dysfunction. He is highly critical of those who believe such disorders are rooted solely in psychology. When he tells you about a man who can't watch his wife strip down without ejaculating all over himself or about a 28-year-old guy who hasn't had an erection for more than a decade because of a damaged artery, you learn how debilitating sexual dysfunction can be.

For Goldstein, the work of a Baylor University urologist, F. Brantley Scott, was the catalyst that took the treatment of sexual dysfunction from the head doctors and brought it into the medical field. "It had to end up in a physician's hands to progress along medical thinking and diagnostics," he explains. Scott, who died in a plane crash in 1991, played an instrumental role in developing the inflatable penile prosthesis, which has been used to treat tens of thousands of patients. The development of this surgically implanted device transformed the landscape of research and opened the field of sexual medicine. "Premature ejaculation, Viagra, orgasm dysfunction, all this stuff ended up in the field of urology," says Goldstein.

By now pharmaceutical engineers have studied the effects on ejaculation of an array of drugs—including neuroleptics, tricyclic antidepressants, opioid agonists, phosphodiestrase inhibitors, sympatholytics, and SSRIs. Beyond drugs, modern researchers have tested rings that wrap around the penis, behavioral techniques such as the stop–start approach, and even virtual-reality programs intended to help men explore their sexual development for events that might have influenced their ejaculatory reflex. Much remains to be learned about the mechanisms of ejaculation, but research bolsters the notion that it is rooted in neurochemical interactions.

"These are people who need help, and we have to be sensitive to their needs and not be rigid," says Goldstein, who directs patients to buy dapoxetine from online pharmacies in foreign countries—a process no more complicated than ordering a book from Amazon.com.

PE Drugs as Lifestyle Drugs
Numerous challenges loom over the success of any drug, and for one that extends intercourse the most significant factors will be pricing and efficacy. "Because premature ejaculation is in such a broad range of patients and doesn't have a correlation with age, it is actually much more in line with a lifestyle drug," says Sarah Terry, of Life Science Analytics. "As a lifestyle drug, it won't be reimbursed by health insurance. People will have to pay out of pocket for it."

Getting men to schedule an appointment to talk about an ostensibly embarrassing disorder and then persuading them to cough up money for treatment will require a costly display of advertising acumen. The battle over direct-to-consumer advertising is nothing new, with one side considering it patient education and the other considering it a tool of deception. Such drug ads are almost exclusive to the United States, coming to the airwaves only in the 1990s. The stakes are now huge: Pfizer has recruited the likes of Bob Dole, Rafael Palmeiro, and NASCAR driver Mark Martin to pitch Viagra. Eli Lilly's ad for Cialis that features a couple in separate bathtubs gazing toward the horizon has been cited by Nielsen as one of the most remembered commercials. As the erection market has grown and competition increased, the ads have became more risqué, sparking complaints and FDA warnings that the drugs are being hawked as party pills. It is unclear how American households will respond when copywriters start churning out euphemisms for *ejaculate*, but chances are there will be some uproar. Any opposition to such ads will give pause to drug companies and research institutes contemplating new ventures in sexual health.

But advertising is essential for any premature ejaculation drug. "We looked at the examples of Viagra, Levitra, and Cialis as a benchmark for the impact of direct-to-consumer advertising," Sarah Terry says. "What we found qualitatively is that, after the launch of Viagra, the marketing of each subsequent product expanded the opportunity of those drugs by nearly 15 to 20 percent each. The amount of marketing out there continued to push the population base that much each time." A similar pattern will presumably emerge with premature ejaculation drugs. The market will swell by millions with each additional approval letter the FDA mails.

Some experts see the real problem as the imposition of normative structures on what is a variable phenomenon. Dr. Leonore Tiefer, associate professor of psychiatry at New York University, is in the vanguard of a movement to undermine the quantification of sexual function. She admits that a drug to delay ejaculation can be useful to some but says there is no such thing as premature ejaculation, and efforts to create drugs to treat it are disingenuous. Sex, Tiefer says, is more like dancing than digestion.

"Fundamentally, being fat or thin is a matter of live variation throughout history and culture," she says. "The same thing is true of coming quickly or not, having a hard erection when you're 60 or not. There's a great deal of variability. To try to stuff it into some simple-minded bottom line is to deny the reality of sex."

Michael Perelman, the New York psychologist, says ejaculatory latency is just another human characteristic, similar to blue eyes, best plotted along a skewed distribution curve. He would like to see the definition of premature ejaculation divided into four categories of severity: when a man can't enter the vagina, when sex lasts less than a minute, when sex lasts one to two minutes, and when it lasts two to four minutes. Perelman reasons that the average physician will see people who consider themselves to be suffering from premature ejaculation who last more than one minute but not as long as they would like to.

Remember that Brendan was nearing two minutes that night in New York. We don't know if he ever felt in control, but distress certainly reared its head. No doctor can fully answer Susan's question as to what the fuck was wrong with Brendan, and no drug can address the underlying factors that determine how long he lasts on any given occasion.

If Brendan had popped a pill that night, would he have been treating a disease or just enhancing an aspect of everyday life? Our regulatory system is designed to weigh the risks and benefits of drugs used to treat defined diseases, not to improve our lifestyles. But the line between treatment and enhancement is now more blurred than ever.

"Such uses of pharmaceuticals pose challenges for us as a country," says Perelman. "The challenge is always greater when we talk about sex."

Big Pharma isn't going to shy away from this conversation. It's adept at dictating what's good and what's bad and what is normal and what isn't. Ejaculation won't be an exception.

Atheists Do It Better:
Why Leaving Religion Leads to Better Sex
Greta Christina

Do atheists have better sex? Yes, according to science—more specifically, according to the recently released study "Sex and Secularism."

In January 2011, organizational psychologist Darrel Ray Ed.D. (a psychologist for 30 years and author of *The God Virus* as well as two books on psychology) and Amanda Brown (an undergraduate at the University of Kansas who focuses on sexuality and sex therapy) conducted a sex survey of over 14,500 subjects—atheists, agnostics, and other people in the secular community. The survey looked at religion, atheism, and sex: how religion affects sex, how leaving religion affects sex, whether lifelong atheists feel differently about sex than people who have recently deconverted, and so on. The report—"Sex and Secularism: What Happens When You Leave Religion?"—is on the Internet, and if you want all 46 pages of the naughty details, including the charts and graphs and personal stories, you can download it free; you only have to register on the website.

But if you just want to know the gist: leaving religion improves people's sex lives. A lot.

Atheists and other nonbelievers, as a whole, experience a lot more satisfaction in their sex lives than they did when they were believers. They feel much less guilt about their sex lives and their sexuality. The sexual guilt instilled by so many religions tends to fade, and indeed disappear, when people leave religion—much more thoroughly than you might expect. And, according to the respondents of this study, nonbelievers give their children significantly better sex education than believers do.

Now, when it comes to people's actual sexual behavior, religion doesn't have nearly as much impact as you might think. Religious and nonreligious people have pretty much the same kinds of sex, at pretty much the same age of onset, and at pretty much the same rate. Believers are just as likely to masturbate, watch porn, have oral sex, have sex outside marriage, and so on, as nonbelievers, and they start at about the same ages. So it's not that religious sexual guilt is actually making people abstain from forbidden sexual activity. All it's doing is making people feel crummy about it. And when people leave religion, this crumminess decreases—at a dramatic rate. Believers and atheists are having pretty much the same kinds of sex—but when it comes to the pleasure and satisfaction experienced during this sex, it's like night and day.

Okay. Before anyone squawks, I'll start the squawking myself: there are some demographic problems with this study, and it shouldn't be relied on as the final word on this topic. In particular, the participants in the study aren't statistically representative of the population; they're statistically representative of whoever heard about it on the Internet, and they're disproportionately represented by readers of the hugely popular atheist blog *Pharyngula*. (In fact, in several places throughout the report, the researchers themselves freely acknowledge the limitations of their research.)

But the results of this report are entirely consistent with the results of other research. Lots of other research, both on human sexuality and on religion/atheism. And that makes these results much more plausible. As researcher Darrel Ray told me, "Our data is virtually identical to other national surveys on the basics of when and how people start sexual behavior." (Citations of those surveys are in the report.) Yes, it's virtually impossible to get completely accurate, statistically representative information about human sexuality under any circumstances; there's not really any ethical way to get information about sex other than relying on people's self-reporting, and it's a topic that people tend to, you know, lie about. But on the reliability scale for human sex research, this report seems to rank at the high end.

You might also argue—as I did when I first saw this research—that atheists are often pretty hostile to religion, and they aren't going to give a fair assessment of their sex lives when they were religious. I think this is a valid point, and one that's worth investigating. In fact, I hope this report marks the beginning of research into this topic rather than the end of it; I would be very interested to see studies about how religious people see their sex lives. I would be especially interested to compare the "Sex and Secularism" results to data from people who have converted from one religion to another, and whether they view their sex lives differently in light of their new religion.

But I'd also point out that the atheists who responded to this survey gave answers that were far from homogeneous. Their responses varied depending on which religion they used to belong to and how intensely religious their upbringing was. They ranged from "ZOMG, my sex life totally sucked and now it's beyond awesome—I was blind but now I see" to "Meh, it's a little better, but it's really not all that different." So the idea that this report simply reflects a knee-jerk atheist hostility to religion is worth considering, but it's probably not what's going on here.

So what is going on here? What does this report say, and what is its take-home message—both for believers and atheists?

Atheism Is for Lovers

Here's one take-home message: atheists fuck better. Or rather, atheists have a better time fucking. They feel less guilt about it; they experience more satisfaction with it. And the effect on their sex lives of leaving religion is almost universally positive.

These effects vary with the religion. According to "Sex and Secularism," some religions have a harsher impact on people's sex lives than others. People raised as Mormons and Jehovah's Witnesses, for instance, ranked much higher on the sexual guilt scale than people raised as Buddhists and Episcopalians. And no, we shouldn't just assume that Catholicism is the guiltiest party. In fact, when it comes to which religions make their practitioners feel guilty about sex, Catholicism is pretty much smack in the middle. At the top of the list are Mormonism, Jehovah's Witness, Pentecostal, Seventh-day Adventist, and Baptist. This is just one of many results in this report that run counter to conventional wisdom.

A similar pattern shows up again and again throughout the report. Conservative religions have a much more harmful effect on people's sex lives than more moderate or progressive ones—in terms of guilt, sexual education and information, the ability to experience pleasure, the ability to accept one's sexual identity, and more.

But with only two exceptions—Unitarianism and Judaism—atheists experience less sexual guilt than religious believers of any denomination. On a scale of 1 to 10—1 being no sexual guilt and 10 being extreme sexual guilt—atheists ranked 4.71 and agnostics ranked 4.81. Only Unitarianism and Judaism ranked slightly lower, at 4.14 and 4.48 respectively; all other religions ranked higher in sexual guilt: from 5.88 for Lutherans to 6.34 for Catholics, all the way up to a whopping 8.19 for Mormons.

And sexual guilt doesn't rise only with the conservativeness of the religion. It rises with religiosity, period. The more religious your upbringing is, the worse your sexual guilt is likely to be. Of people raised in very religious homes, 22.5 percent said they were shamed or ridiculed for masturbating (to give just one example), compared to only 5.5 percent of people brought up in the least religious homes. And of people raised in very religious homes, 79.9 percent felt guilty about a specific sexual activity or desire, while among people raised in the least religious and most secular homes, that number drops to 26.3 percent. That's a huge difference.

But one of the most surprising conclusions of this research is that sexual guilt from religion doesn't wreck people's sex lives forever.

According to conventional wisdom—and I will freely admit that I held this conventional wisdom myself—religious guilt about sex continues to torment people long after the religion itself has lost its hold. But according to "Sex and Secularism," that's rarely the case. Once people let go of religion, they report positive experiences of sex, and relative lack of guilt about it, at about the same rate as people who were never religious in the first place.

Ray was surprised by this result as well. (Surprising results—a sign of good science!) "We did think that religion would have residual effects in people after they left," he told me, "but our data did not show this. That was a very pleasant surprise. That is not to say that some people don't continue to experience problems, but the vast majority seem to shake it off and get on with their sexual lives pretty well." So letting go of religion means a rebound into a sex life that's as satisfying, and as guilt-free, as a sex life that was never touched by religion in the first place.

Now, some hard-core religious believers might argue that this isn't a good thing. "People should feel sexual guilt!" they'd argue. "Sex is bad, mmmkay? God doesn't approve. People should feel guilty about it."

But two things are worth pointing out. First of all, the activities studied by this research are, from any rational perspective, morally neutral. This report doesn't consider rape, or nonconsensual voyeurism, or groping people on the subway. It considers masturbation, oral sex, nonmarital sex, homosexuality: sex acts and sexualities that are consensual, egalitarian, reasonably safe, and harmless to society. The taboos against them are just that: taboos. If there ever were any solid practical or moral reasons behind them, they're buried in the mists of history. And different religions have entirely different sets of these sexual taboos: One religion may denounce certain sex acts and accept others, while another accepts Column B but denounces Column A. If God has a message for us about who and how he wants us to boff, he's not being very clear about it.

Maybe more to the point, religion has essentially no effect on people's actual sexual behavior, according to the report. Atheists and believers engage in the same practices, at basically the same rate, starting at essentially the same age. We're all doing pretty much the same stuff. Believers just feel worse about it. As Ray told me, "Our data shows that people feel very guilty about their sexual behavior when they are religious, but that does not stop them: it just makes them feel bad. Of course, they have to return to their religion to get forgiveness. It's as if the church gives you the disease, then offers you a fake cure." So the argument that religious sexual guilt is good because it polices immoral sexual behavior fails on two fronts. The sexual behavior it's policing isn't actually immoral—and the policing is almost entirely ineffective.

Oh, by the way—this improvement in people's sex lives when they leave religion isn't just about relieving sexual guilt. The improvement shows up in many aspects of their sex lives, such as their willingness to share sex fantasies with a partner, for example. Most important, it shows up in people's assessments of their sex lives overall. This is truest of the people who were heavily religious before their deconversion. On a scale of 1 to 10—1 being a sex life that is much worse after leaving religion, 10 being a sex life that is much improved—people who had the most religious lives before averaged a very high 7.81; 61.6 percent gave an answer of 8, 9, or 10—"greatly improved." People with little or no religion in their life before they became atheists mostly report that their sex lives didn't change that much.

In fact, for the handful of atheists who reported that their sex lives worsened when they left religion—2.2 percent of participants—almost all tell the same story: their sex lives got worse because—well, to put it bluntly, their partners or potential partners were still religious, and now that they were atheists, they weren't getting any. Their spouses got upset because they'd become atheists; their pool of potential sex partners dried up. As one respondent commented, "My wife said to me, 'How can I sleep with someone who doesn't share my faith?'" Another, somewhat more waggishly, said, "When I was a Christian I could lay any girl in church, now that I am an atheist, they won't even talk to me."

Perhaps one of the most powerful messages in this report—if one of the least surprising—is the decidedly negative effect of religion on sexual education and information. People raised in more strongly religious homes ranked the quality of their sex education as significantly worse than people raised in less religious homes: 2.4 on a 5-point scale, as opposed to 3.2 from the less religious folks. And the more-religious kids were less likely to get sex information from their parents than the less-religious ones—13.5 percent, as opposed to 38.2 percent—and more likely to get it from personal sexual experience and pornography.

In case the irony escapes anyone, let me hammer it home. The highly religious, "family values" crowd are more likely to get their sexual information from porn and fooling around—while the less religious folks are more likely to talk to their parents. And in case anyone is wondering why sex education was included in this study on sexual happiness: accurate sex education and information has been consistently shown to be one of the cornerstones of a happy, satisfying sex life.

Which, again, atheists are a lot more likely to have.

Happy Endings

So what does this research say to believers?

Well, the most obvious message would be: come on in—the water's fine.

In debates with atheists, many believers argue for religion on the basis of how good it makes them feel. They argue that religion is emotionally useful, psychologically useful, socially useful: that religion gives people a sense of meaning, moral guidance, comfort in hard times, etc. It's an argument that drives many atheists up a tree—myself included—since it has absolutely nothing to do with whether religion is, you know, true. (Believing in Santa Claus might make kids happy and better-behaved, but you wouldn't argue that people should keep putting cookies by the fireplace on Christmas Eve well into their adult years.)

But if this report is to be believed, this usefulness argument is conclusively shown to be bogus—even on its own terms. At least when it comes to sex. (It's probably bogus when it comes to the rest of our lives as well—or rather, it would be bogus if our society didn't privilege religious belief and treat atheism with bigotry and contempt. Countries with higher rates of atheism actually have higher levels of happiness and social functioning than more religious countries. But I digress.)

Religion doesn't make people happier. Not in the sack, anyway. Religion makes people less happy. Leaving religion makes people happier. There's no reason to hang on to beliefs you don't actually believe in and that don't actually make sense to you, just because you can't imagine a happy and fulfilling life without them. We know that leaving religion can be a scary and painful process—but once it's behind you, life is good. And the sex is great. Come on in. The water's fine.

And what does this report say to atheists?

This report, people, is our sales pitch.

Again, I will make this very clear: The fact that atheists fuck better has no bearing whatsoever on whether atheism is correct. And atheists should not pretend that it does.

But when believers make the argument from utility—when they argue that religion is important and necessary because it makes people happy—we don't have to just tear our hair out and say, "Does not! Does not!" We can print out this report and hand it to them with a smile.

A satisfied smile.

To All the Butches I Loved between 1995 and 2005: An Open Letter about Selling Sex, Selling Out, and Soldiering On

Amber Dawn

You were a set of sturdy boys in well-worn Carhartt jeans and rock T-shirts. Rough scrubbed, each one of you, from your Bryl-creemed hair to your polished black jump boots. You rode bellowing 1970s muscle bikes, drove cars with duct-tape interiors, walked with practiced swaggers. You could hold your own at the pool table and in the kitchen—cooking your mamas' comfort-food recipes. You played "Ace of Spades" on electric guitar and hemmed your own pants. You spent your days painting six-bedroom houses in Shaughnessy, tending to show-jumping horses, keeping university grounds, or otherwise soiling your fingers. You were evolved renditions of the very boy a small-town slut like me was expected to wind up with. But unlike that probable boyfriend, you were a feminist, you rejected the status quo with much greater consideration than it rejected you, and you didn't leave me a knocked-up single mother-to-be. I couldn't possibly have told you enough how truly remarkable you were.

To all the butches I loved between 1995 and 2005, there is a consequential and heartfelt queue of things I never said to you. Blame booze or youth, frequently practiced self-flagellation, homophobia, or a brew of stinking societal influences for me holding my tongue. What matters now is that I put some honest words to our past and—if the graces allow—that you will hear me.

If the details are a blur (and I don't blame you if they are), let me remind you that I was your girl, your mommy, your headache, or your heart song (depending on my mood). On a good day I wrote poetry, walked rescue dogs, or led survivors' support groups at the women's center. I'd all but quit rush drugs, but on a bad day I drank like a fancy fighting betta fish in a small bowl. I spent my nights gliding around softly lit massage parlors in a pair of flitter-pink stilettos. Personal economics informed my femme identity. My transition took place in prudent increments: I grew my neon-orange dyke hair into a mane of bleached blonde; I shaved my armpits and pussy; I dropped down to 100 pounds, and, in effect, I learned to indulge the tastes of men with money to spend. When the business was good, I made more in an hour than you did all week.

This is where my overdue disclosures begin. Whenever I picked up the dinner tab or put gas in your tank, we'd both swallow a quiet shame. I might have mumbled something aloof like, "Easy come, easy go," handling the neatly folded bills with the same cool discretion as my male customers did when they paid me.

For a good long time, I positioned this shame entirely in a have-and-have-not credo. I believed that all my shame came from the very same grounds as my pride: my humble class background.

I've since realized that this summation is too easy.

You and I and just about everyone we knew were salt-of-the-earth folk. Salt of the earth meets pervert, that is, on account of our being the kind of kinky, tough-love queers that set us apart from our back-home birth families. Ours was an elbow-grease, adult-children-of-alcoholics, there-ain't-no-such-thing-as-a-free-lunch butch-femme. That's right, let's say it again. Our was a damaged-goods, bitter-pill, better-luck-next-time butch-femme. We were cut from the same threadbare cloth, and we wore it well. Our world was filled with modest yet revered codes and traditions. When guests came over, they were offered mismatched kitchen chairs to sit on. If there was whiskey in the cupboard, it was either Jim or Jack. Clothing was swapped. Tools were shared. There were logging-road camping trips and back-alley bonfires. We danced like crazy in creaky-floored rental rec centers and declining dance halls; we'd make the air hot and muggy, the old wood floors stickier than flypaper. And in the dark safe corners of the night, we fucked with our fists, teeth, and hearts like we were indestructible. This was our behind-the-eight-ball butch-femme. I was never ashamed of it.

The shame I felt came from sex work. There it is, as bare-faced as it can be. Don't get me wrong, I still wear my feminist-slut badge. This isn't some dubious argument over the merits of waiting tables for minimum wage versus the formidable money-making potential of prostitution. Morals are not being reexamined here. I'm not moving from "camp empowerment" to "camp victim"—such dichotomies are far too short-sighted to sum up sex workers. What I'm coming out about is that sex work changed my relationship with being a working-class femme and, in turn, my relationship with you, my butch lovers.

Sometimes you tried to talk about it. I want to thank you for being brave enough to speak up, even though you didn't always say the right thing. I remember waking up one morning to your big green eyes. You had been watching me sleep since sunrise, adoringly at first, the way smitten lovers do, then your thoughts took a turn and you began to wonder, How the heck is this my girlfriend? Fake tan, synthetic hair weave, fake, long airbrushed fingernails; you said that lying beside me felt "surreal." I suppose I looked like a poster child for the beauty myth we had been warned about in our early 90s feminist education. I looked like the kind of femme who is dubbed "high maintenance" or "a princess"—indeed these labels were used to describe me—though the reality was that sex work had only made me tougher and more fiercely independent. Still, there wasn't anything punk rock or edgy, humble, or even queer about my exterior femme persona. I pretty much looked like I belonged in a commercial for a chat line or a diet pill. The familiar fit of you and me (your butch and my femme) had been disrupted. Had I sold out our butch-femme codes? Had I snuck the bourgeois "other" into our bed?

"I make more money when I look like this." How frequently I used this disclaimer. It was the fractured thinking I employed as a sex worker: there was the persona and then there was the real me. But, as I've already mentioned, easy dichotomies fall short. As with my appearance, sex work began to shape my life. Prostitution money paid for my liberal arts degree, an MFA in creative writing. If I was going to be the college-student-by-day, working-girl-by-night cliché, I was determined to average at least a 4.0—even if it meant turning a date with a dental student during lunch break so I could pay for my biology tutor that same afternoon. I was raised with the principle of sacrifice; if I was going to obtain the things that my class background hadn't afforded me, I figured I was bound to suffer at least a little.

While I'd grown somewhat accustomed to grappling with the personal sacrifices that came with sex work, witnessing your inner conflict was an entirely different challenge. Although we both agreed in theory that my job ought to be treated like any other line of work, if your boss called to offer you an extra shift, our biggest dilemma was whether the overtime would cut into our upcoming scheduled dates. "Baby, you don't mind, do you?" was all you needed to say, conversation closed. In contrast, entire nights seemed to be ruined when my madam called to ask me to take a last-minute client. As I'd whisper into my cell phone, I witnessed your face stiffen. Eventually, the sound of my ringtone alone was cause for pause.

I never had to lie to my friends about what you did for a living. "She's a carpenter" or a "welder-in-training," I boasted. These were strong, rugged, and proudly butch professions. For you, telling people your girlfriend was a sex worker was a crapshoot, at best. Of course, I was out to our close mutual friends. Others were told a half-truth: that I was a stripper rather than a full-fledged, blow job–performing prostitute. This explanation spared you from uttering an outright lie and also from making your buddies uncomfortable or concerned. What kind of man dates a prostitute? A tyrant, a pimp, or a broken man who can't take care of his woman. Our radical queer values didn't protect us from these stigmas. "I wish I could protect you" was another brave thing that you frequently said to me. I took what comfort I could in this sentiment and let you wrap your arms around me a little tighter. This tender statement, however, affirmed how truly uncomfortable you were with sex work and, worse still, how uncomfortable you were that my work made you feel powerless. Butches aren't supposed to feel powerless. I was inadvertently de-butching you. And, as a femme who believes (and celebrates) that her role as a femme is to make her butch feel like one hell of a butch, I was de-femming myself, too.

Confessions don't come any harder than this one: sex work changed the way I fucked.

I remember the first time I refused to kneel for you. We were making out at one of our fuck spots, between a row of high-school portables a few blocks from your house. You took out your cock, ran your thumb along my bottom lip, and yanked my hair as you did when you wanted me on the ground. It was Friday night. The next day was my regular Saturday shift, when all the big-tipping clients visited the massage parlor, and I couldn't risk having my knees scraped like a "cheap whore." It might have messed with my money. Moreover, I refused to reveal the real me at work. My work persona didn't have scraped knees (or welts or hickeys, etc.).

The simplest, sexiest diversion would have been to spit on your cock and lift my skirt. Instead, I stood there frozen in that inciting moment when I realized that keeping my real life and work neatly separated was impossible; it was failing at every opportunity. Sex work was not simply coating the surface of my body like a topcoat of glitter nail polish. It had sunk in.

We could playfully liken my appearance to a drag queen's. My money financed more than a few good times together. But we met an impasse when the impact of sex work entered our bedroom. Setting boundaries around scraped knees was only a preview to long and recurring phases when I couldn't be touched at all. Contrary to your fantasies and my own, I wasn't an inexhaustible source of amorous coos and sighs. My pussy was not an eternal femme spring, always wet and ready. The image of the coquette was critical to our relationship. It was critical to who I was as a femme. I hadn't chosen the saccharine country classic "Touch

Your Woman" by Dolly Parton (my working-class femme role model) as a mantra for nothing! Who was I, as a femme, if I couldn't offer my body to you, my butch lovers, as a touchstone, a safe haven of hotness, a soft-skinned, sweet-mouthed reminder that who we were was right and good?

A bigger question: what the heck did sex between us look like if I wasn't going to spread my legs anymore? Most of you had your own set of complex raw spots—as our generation of butches with hard-knock pasts often do. I'd spent my younger femme years devotedly learning about and responding to the nuanced body language and boundaries of butches. Suddenly, it was all I could do to keep up with my own changing limits and body issues.

For a while I tried on "stone femme" as an identity. In many ways, this label protected me and made me feel powerful. It also became a regular topic for dissection in our small community. "A stone femme, meaning a femme who loves stone butches?" I was asked repeatedly.

"No, I mean I myself am stone." I'd say. "I don't let lovers touch me."

"Hmm." I got a lot of doubtful "hmms" in response, as if I were speaking in riddles.

Ultimately, changes to the way I fucked meant we both had to reinvent the codes and traditions of the butch-femme bedroom as we knew them, which under different circumstances might have been a fun task, but the possibilities weren't as discernible as the losses. We didn't ask "Could we...?" as often as we asked "Why can't we...?"

Let's just skip the berating part, where I say, "I admit I wasn't always an easy woman to stand beside." Let's move right to the part where I simply thank you for doing so. If you've hung on and heard me this far, then please let me finish this letter by explaining exactly what it is I am thanking you for.

You were adaptable. You tried really darn hard to be adaptable. Most of the time this only made you about as flexible as a flagpole, but I noticed you bend and knew that you did it for me. I remember the time you let me strap it on and be the first femme to fuck you. It ranks quite high up in my list of all-time favorite memories. Later, you gloated to your butch buddies, "She's more 'butch' than me between the sheets." To my surprise, comradely arm punching and shared stupid grins followed this admission. It made me wonder if you needed that fuck (and those that followed) as desperately as I did. Maybe you needed a damaged-goods, stone femme like me to ask you to become something besides the ever-infallible butch top you were accustomed to being.

Likewise, maybe you needed to cry with me during those rare times when you resisted the urge to take up the emotional reins and say "Baby, don't cry" or "It will be okay." This was a delicate and extraordinary space, where we both unabashedly cried together. For me, it was the emotional antithesis of the wordless reactive shame I often felt but lacked the guts or words to talk about. Thank you for sharing this space with me.

There were many moments when I doubted myself during those years—hazardous moments, like brushes with bad clients, when yours were the strong arms in which I sought respite. There were also many instances when I lacked the confidence to walk with dignity into a university classroom or a square job interview, moments when I was tempted to blow my ho money by going on benders because climbing the class ladder was terrifying. Thank you for loving me the way you knew best. Your big calloused hands held me strong to this life. You still took me dancing until our clothes were soaked through with sweat. You popped Heart's *Greatest Hits* in your car stereo, and we drove the back roads singing "Crazy on You" in comically awful disharmony. You called me "old lady" and "beautiful" and "your girl." You taught me that butch-femme wasn't about dress codes, the gendered skills we'd acquired, or jobs we held, or even about who bent over in the bedroom. At the crux of it all, our butch-femme traditions were about creating a place that was distinctly ours. Again and again you brought me to this home, this shelter from external pressures, this asylum from troubled pasts and uncertain futures. Thank you for assuring me that I always had a remarkable, shameless place.

I Want You to Want Me

Hugo Schwyzer

Like countless American children, I grew up hearing the nursery rhyme in which little boys are characterized as "snips and snails and puppy-dog tails" while girls are "sugar and spice and everything nice." As a small boy very attached to our pet dachshund, I thought puppy-dog tails were a fine thing indeed, but the point of the rhyme wasn't lost on me. Boys were dirty, girls were clean and pure.

We're raised in a culture that both celebrates and pathologizes male "dirtiness." On the one hand, boys were and are given license to be louder, rowdier, and more sexual. We're expected to get our hands dirty, to rip our pants, and get covered in stains. We enjoy a freedom to be dirty that goes hand in hand with the expectation that we are in a state of perpetual craving for women's bodies. Even now, too many girls grow up shamed for wanting to be dirty. And if men's bodies are dirty, then to lust after them is to be dirty as well.

For many guys, growing up with the right to be dirty is accompanied by the realization that many people find the male body repulsive. In sixth grade, the same year that puberty hit me with irrevocable force, I had an art teacher, Mr. Blake. (This dates me: few public middle schools have art teachers anymore.) I'll never forget his solemn declaration that great artists all acknowledged that the female form was more beautiful than the male. He made a passing crack that "no one wants to see naked men, anyway"— and the whole class laughed. "Ewwww," a girl sitting next to me said, evidently disgusted at the thought of a naked boy.

In time, I discovered that Mr. Blake was wrong about this so-called artistic consensus. But it took me a lot longer to unlearn the damage done by remarks like his and by the conventional wisdom of my childhood. I came into puberty convinced both that my male body was repulsive and that the girls for whom I longed were flawless. (I still remember how floored I was at 16, when the lovely classmate on whom I had a crush farted while I was sitting next to her in German class. I had sincerely believed until that moment that women didn't pass gas.)

A year later, in my first sexual relationship, I was convinced that my girlfriend found my body physically repellent. I could accept that girls liked and wanted sex, but I figured that what my girlfriend liked was how I made her feel in spite of how my body must have appeared to her. Though I trusted that she cared for me, the idea that she—or any other woman—could want this sweaty, smelly, fumbling flesh was still unthinkable. What made her want to have sex with me, I assumed, was a combination of two things: her love for me (which trumped her "natural" disgust), and my own skill.

Not long after that first relationship broke up, I went through what would be the first of many periods of promiscuity. I had sex with a series of women and men. I knew I wasn't gay, but I wasn't inflexibly straight either; though I could only experience romantic feelings for women, I was turned on by both sexes. Count me in the camp of those who believe that sexual fluidity isn't just for women; authentic male bisexuality is far from a myth. But my own bisexuality seemed to mirror the "Mr. Blake problem"—though I was physically drawn to both sexes, I found women more sexually alluring. Whether that was because I wasn't really bi or because I bought into what I'd been taught about the comparative undesirability of the male body, I wasn't sure.

I established a pattern in high school that would stay with me for years. While the women I had sex with were always within a year or two of my own age, almost all the men I slept with were a decade or two my senior. With women, I was usually the pursuer; with men, I was the pursued. And while I often liked the actual sex with women better, I loved the way my male lovers made me feel wanted.

I grew up on the Monterey Peninsula in the 1980s, home to the now-shuttered Fort Ord and a number of other military installations. Most of the guys I slept with when I was in high school were soldiers or sailors or airmen. One Friday night, a few weeks before my 18th birthday, an older man picked me up on a street corner. I think his name was James; he was a master sergeant. He was certainly one of the oldest guys I ever fucked during my teens, perhaps in his mid-forties.

James was huge—everywhere. When he took off his clothes in the dimly lit Fremont Boulevard motel room, I was turned on and terrified at the same time, and by the same thing. I looked at his cock and his muscles and his tattoos and thought to myself, *He could rape me if he wanted. He could kill me with his bare hands.* And then he started to take off my clothes, and my fear evaporated.

This giant of a man whispered sweet, sexy words as he pulled off my shirt, shoes, and jeans. I'd never been undressed by a lover before; I stood submissive, passive, open-mouthed. I shifted my weight to help him slide off my clothes, but made no other move. I listened.

I'd been a clumsy, awkward kid. I'd struggled with a bad case of acne early in my teens. I was just coming out of a chubby stage. And on top of that, I still had damn Mr. Blake's words in my head. *Who wants to see a naked man, anyway?*

James wanted. James wanted to see me, to touch me, to kiss every inch of me. And as he made his way down my body, he praised everything his hands and lips touched. The master sergeant had quite a tongue on him, and he used it effectively.

Standing there under the heat of his gaze and his touch, I felt a rush of elation and relief so great it made me cry. The sex I had with him was based less on my own desire than on my own colossal gratitude for how he had made me feel with his words and his gaze. As we lay on the motel bed, this man ran his fingers across every inch of my body, murmuring flattery of a kind I had never heard from a woman's lips. As I lay beneath him on that lumpy motel mattress, the dim light of the TV flickering in the corner, he said the words I can still hear nearly 30 years on:

You're so hot you make me want to come.

I remember the next sound: my own gasp, my own lust and pain and gratitude mixing together. How different his words were from my ex-girlfriend's gentle reassurance: "Hugo, you make me feel so good." While she had praised my technique, James praised my body's desirability. And I realized how much I craved exactly that kind of affirmation. James didn't just give me that validation for one night. He changed how I saw my own skin and my own maleness.

I don't want to suggest that straight women don't lust, and that only gay or bi men are vocal about their strong sexual craving for male bodies. As I got older, I met women who were more confident about expressing desire, and discovered that it wasn't only gay or bi men who craved the male body. And I came to see that our cultural myths about desire hurt everyone. We shame women for wanting, and we shame men for wanting to be wanted. We still have too many Mr. Blakes out there, giving that same destructive message that no one wants (or should want) the dirty, disgusting male body. (See the recent discussion on a professional photographers' website about the unattractiveness of naked men viewed "from the front."[1])

Acknowledging Men's Longing to Be Admired

Though our culture often also teaches women that their bodies are dirty (particularly because of menstruation), we make it clear that men "naturally" crave and desire them. Teaching women that their bodies have great power over men creates a huge problem for women. By putting the focus on managing male desire, women are taught to ignore or suppress their own desires. That's a loss for women, and it's a loss for men.

Before I started doing men's work two decades ago, I wondered if my longing to be wanted was perhaps unique to me. I quickly found out otherwise, as I heard this topic come up again and again, often charged with great pain. So many straight men have no experience of sensing a gaze of outright longing. Even many men who are wise in the world and in relationships, who know that their wives or girlfriends love them, do not know what it is to be admired for their bodies and their looks. They may know what it is to be relied upon, they may know what it is to bring another to ecstasy with their touch, but they don't know what it is to be found not only aesthetically pleasing to the eye, but worthy of longing. *And they want to know.*

The hurt and rage that men feel as a result of having no sense of their own attractiveness has very real and destructive consequences. While both men and women often struggle to trust a partner's affirmation of their desirability, men are more likely to externalize that struggle as anger at women. Men's belief that "women only pretend to want sex" is at the root of a lot of male rage, a rage that wives and girlfriends and lovers are forced to deal with all too often.

This isn't women's problem to solve; it's not as if it's women's job to start stroking yet another aspect of the male ego. The answer lies in creating a new vocabulary for desire, empowering women as well as men to gaze, expanding our own sense of what is good and beautiful, aesthetically and erotically pleasing. That's hard stuff, but it's worth the effort. I have known what it is to believe myself repulsive, and also what it is to hear that I am not only wanted but desirable—for how I appear as well as how I act. That was precious indeed, and far too few men have known it.

Endnotes
_____

1 http://digital-photography-school.com/forum/general-chit-chat/144038-why-do-nude-photos-men-bother-me.html

Grief, Resilience, and My 66th Birthday Gift
Joan Price

During my extreme grief after Robert died, I cried all day. "I cried" is such an understatement: I wailed, I screamed, I keened. I exploded in great, ripping waves of crying that felt like I was vomiting tears uncontrollably from my gut. I understood the term "a broken heart"—it felt like my heart was literally breaking, sawed to pieces by a huge, merciless, serrated knife while an elephant kicked me in the chest.

What does this have to do with sex? Nothing—and everything. For the first months, I didn't have sex at all, not even with myself. Grief buried my sex drive, except that in my memory, I made love with Robert all day long, celebrating our erotic highs, his beautiful dancer's body, his touches, his howls of pleasure—and my own.

★ ★ ★

Robert and I met in the line dance class I teach. I was 57 and he was celebrating his 64th birthday on the evening he wandered in, looking for a new place to dance, and altered my life. I was fired by lust immediately, especially after he started to dance, his gracefulness and mobile hips revealing a lifetime of dance training.

I couldn't take my eyes off this sexy, white-haired man with ocean-blue eyes and a "touch this, please" tuft of curly white chest hair peeking from the *V* of his shirt. I imagined holding him, unbuttoning his shirt, nuzzling that chest hair.

Nine months later ("I don't get into sex casually," he had told me), I got to do just that. I nuzzled his chest hair, his head hair, his belly hair, his pubic hair. Even now, three years after his death, I can feel the soft, springy texture in my memory, as vivid as the last time I touched him.

Our lust and our profound love thrilled us. We scheduled whole afternoon sex dates, reveling in the power of our aging bodies and minds to rise to exhilarating heights. It was the best sex of our lives.

Was it the same as 20-year-old sex? Not even close—we weren't driven by the biological urge to reproduce, but by the drive to bond and touch and share pleasure. And our bodies didn't go into ready mode right away. In fact, my arousal time was so long that at first I was embarrassed. Silly me, I even apologized to Robert for the amount of stimulation I needed.

"I don't care if it takes three weeks," he told me, "as long as I can get up sometimes to change positions and get something to eat." His humor, creativity, and enjoyment of his own physicality—combined with our deep love—made our sex soar and roar.

We loved. I wrote a book about senior sex, Robert painted

beautiful art, we moved in together, we married.

Robert died of cancer exactly seven years after our first kiss.

"Can you see yourself dating again, getting in a relationship again, having sex again?" my friends asked me as I mourned Robert. Even curious readers of my sex and aging book and blog would ask me this.

At first, I said no. I had found and lost my great love—no one could follow that. My sex life with Robert, the love of my life, had been so dynamic, so passionate, so thrilling that his loss felt like the end to everything. Yes, I was still interested in sex, but more as a writer and sex educator than in my personal life.

Then, amazingly, about six months into my grieving, I started to feel stirrings. I found myself feeling turned on by men who radiated that enticing combination of sexuality and gentleness. I didn't act on those feelings, but I admit I was surprised and happy that I was feeling them. I didn't feel the need to satisfy the urge—it was enough to marvel at still being able to feel it. We human beings are amazingly resilient.

I remember having a dream at that time that I was responding sexually to a fully dressed, sexy man who was pressing his aroused self against me. I awoke, excited and filled with wonder. "I'm still alive!" I said aloud.

A year and a half after Robert's death, I prepared to face my 66th birthday alone. I longed for a man's touch, but still hadn't felt comfortable enough—or attracted enough—to welcome another man into my body. I wanted to be aroused and I wanted to or-gasm from a man's touch—but (was this selfish?) I wanted the pleasure without giving back just yet. There were men in my life who offered their services, but it didn't seem fair to take and not give, and a real relationship was too complicated. I feared I would dissolve into tears if I made love with a new man.

I wondered, though, could I *hire* this pleasure? Men bought "happy endings" easily—could I?

I started looking on the Internet. Most ads and websites were sleazy and scary enough to make me run for cover. Then someone I trusted recommended Sunyata:

Our Sacred Session may involve sensual, intimate touch—unconditionally loving your body with sacred, sensual, and erotic touch that catalyses holistic energetic shifts and nurtures your soul to vibrant life. This touch may stimulate you and result in a climax of pleasure—however, the goal of orgasm is not the focus of the Sacred Session.

I read Sunyata's website over and over, pausing over these words. Then I wrote this email to a man I had never met:

> Sunyata, I lost my beloved husband to cancer. I have been celibate for a year and a half (exactly, as of today), despite being a writer about sexuality. Although my toys enable me to keep my sexuality strong, I have been longing to be the recipient of a respectful, gentle, erotic massage with no body parts off limits. Your Erotic Enrichment, as described on your website, seems to fit what I am seeking.

He emailed back, then we had a phone conversation. We made an appointment for my 66th birthday.

Me? Hire someone I've never met to give me an "erotic massage," with every intention that it will lead to orgasm? Yes. I did it, I loved it, and it still brings a smile to my face and a tingle to my nether parts remembering it. (Now I'm really shocking my family.)

Brave? Maybe. Typical of me? Absolutely not—I had never done anything like this before. Foolhardy? It didn't seem so. He was recommended by someone I knew, and his website and client references seemed professional and impressive. Sure, a bad guy could construct an appealing website and concoct convincing testimonials, but would a bad guy go to the trouble of claiming to be a Certified Tantric Healer, Reiki Master, and Universal Life Church Minister? Would a bad guy even know what these terms meant?

Face it—it's a fantasy of ours: a pair of skilled hands focused on giving erotic pleasure, no reciprocation expected (or allowed), nonsleazy, all pleasure, orgasms included. No, no, I wasn't buying sex, Sunyata assured me. I wasn't buying any *outcome*. I was simply hiring his services. And if I happened to get carried away experiencing his services—these are my words, not his—every response would be accepted and celebrated.

I still missed Robert like crazy. I had been with Robert exclusively for our seven years together, and his face, hands, and body were the images that stirred my fantasy life when I aroused myself. I pictured Robert as he was through all but the last months of our relationship, vital and strong: a dancer's body, an artist's hands, a lover's smile. I imagined that he was the one touching me when I touched myself. I heard his murmurs of love. I saw his body responding to my touch. I felt his kiss.

And now I wondered: If another man were to touch me intimately, would I even be able to respond?

Sunyata seemed a safe way to find out. I would pay his fee, lie on his massage table, and receive his full attention for two hours.

Sunyata started our session with a discussion, seated on a couch in the massage room, both of us fully clothed. (He would remain so; I would not.) He asked me about what brought me there, and listened compassionately to my story. He explained the basic premise of the massage, which was a way to move Tantric energy (I think—I admit I was too nervous to retain what he was saying). He explained that he was offering his service to honor me, and it would not be reciprocal.

"The session's intent is to provide service in one direction—to you, my guest," he explained. "You are welcome to touch me in nonerogenous areas of my body for connection and emotional support, but not to engage with my eros or my genitals. My sexual desire or need for gratification does not enter the space of our sacred session."

In other words, I was to get naked, climb on the table, relax, and receive.

But would *my* sexual desire and need for gratification "enter the space?" I couldn't ask directly, because I knew we were hovering on the edge of what was legal. I concentrated on listening between the lines.

"I focus on being present with your desire and what wants to release or be revealed," he continued. That answered my question.

It started out as a traditional massage, relaxing and unhurried. Traditional except that he didn't skip my breasts as nonsexual massage practitioners do. I felt my nipples harden to his touch. I arched my back in response to his gliding hands—strong, sure, gentle.

Would Robert approve of what I was doing? I couldn't help flashing on this, which put me on the verge of tears. No, he wouldn't approve or understand. But Robert would never touch me again, and I had to find my own way to reclaim the sensual and sexual life within me. I pulled my awareness back to the present, the gentle touch of this stranger offering pleasure, as much pleasure as I wanted. And I wanted it.

As Sunyata continued massaging me for a very long time (an hour, maybe?—time stopped), my whole body and brain began to quiver in anticipation. I felt my body rise and fall with his touch, his rhythm in sync with mine. I kept my eyes closed, focusing on the sensation.

I parted my thighs, and I could feel my own heat drawing his hands closer to my pleasure center. Finally, his hand cupped my vulva and waited. I rocked into his hand, my clitoris on fire. His hand moved expertly, slowly, gently, waiting for my response with each movement.

"May I touch your yoni?" he asked quietly. Oh yes, oh yes, oh yes. Fingers entered me, slick with massage oil. He massaged me slowly and gently, inside and out, as if his hands had known me forever. He and I were the ocean—timeless, our rhythm primordial and certain.

I gave myself up to Sunyata's expert hands, and the ocean soared and roared in crashing waves of pleasure. Wild sensations, the culmination of a year and a half of grief and longing. I laughed. I cried. I laughed again.

His massage turned quiet again, relaxing me after my wild ride. As he stroked me, my arousal started to rise again. Though in "normal" life, one orgasm is absolutely fulfilling and plenty for me, his hands responded to my surge and—more quickly this time—the waves crashed again.

"You must love your job," I mumbled to Sunyata as I quieted finally.

"I love my job," he said. I pictured him smiling but I didn't manage to open my eyes to find out.

My birthday erotic massage from a gentle stranger changed something in me. It showed me that I was still a responsive, fully sexual woman, getting ready to emerge from the cocoon of mourning into reexperiencing life. I realized that one big reason I ended up on Sunyata's massage table was so that I could get ready to reenter the world.

Sometimes Robert seems to talk to me. I ask him, "Are you really talking to me, or am I making this up?" and he replies, "It doesn't matter." As I approach the third anniversary of his death, I receive this message as clearly as if his voice utters it:

> Baby, when I was alive I wanted you all to myself. I needed reassurance that in loving you so much I wasn't risking losing myself by losing you. I wasn't sure I could give you enough to make you happy.
>
> I can't make you happy now. I can't hold you except in your memory and sometimes in dreams.
>
> You don't need to ask my permission to live your life fully and zestfully. Or to share that love and lust in you with another.
>
> You have so much life in you, sweetheart, so much love to give.
>
> Give it.
>
> If you need my blessing, you have it.
>
> Love always,
>
> Robert

Although I still miss Robert every time I breathe in or out, I know I'll have a lover again, and it will be good. I know I can't replace the love I shared with Robert and I'm not looking for that—but I do need to stay vibrant and alive. Nurturing my sexual self is a part of being fully alive that I will embrace.

Latina Glitter
Rachel Rabbit White

The stars of the oldest Latino drag show in the United States admit that the term *drag* is a bit of a misnomer for their show—because the queens of this stage are not the usual men in drag you expect to find but male-to-female transgender performers.

Ketty Teanga is high femme. It was clear from the time she was nine years old, trotting in her mom's heels. But it wasn't until age 15 that she decided to embrace being a woman. Ketty was still living as a man, but started dancing in a drag show. It was the 1960s in Puerto Rico. "The shows were spectacular, very famous. But back then it was not femme, you had to take off your wig at the end of the show to prove you were a man." The climate was rough: "In Puerto Rico, the police would stop you if you were in drag. We would get out at four a.m. from a show, in street clothes, but they would press a napkin on our face to see if we had on makeup. If we did, they would arrest us right there."

Hers is a story we don't often see in the media. When trans people do get a rare spotlight, it's often the stories of white trans people. Richard Rodriguez, Associate Professor in the Latina/Latino Studies program at the University of Illinois, explains, "As anyone who grew up in a Latino community will tell you, there are always LGBT people around. Sometimes they are accepted and sometimes they aren't. What I find, however, is that LGBT Latinas and Latinos may find more acceptance among Latinos than white queers."

Decades later, Teanga is still a (transgender) drag performer. Her home is covered in glittering dresses, glossy photographs, and LGBT awards. Teanga started what is known as the oldest Latino drag show in the country, at La Cueva in Chicago, where only Spanish is spoken. But it's not a "drag show" in the usual sense—all the performers are MTF transgender women. While Teanga no longer performs, she can still be seen at the bar 4:00 a.m., watching the new crop of glittery performers. "I am gonna die in the show. That's my life," she says, her voice hoarse.

While so much has changed since Teanga's day, when each performer tells her story, the themes are similar to Teanga's. "I would play with my sister in Mexico. We played tea party and made cookies with sugar, pretending to be famous sisters and artists. My mom would get mad because I would wear her dresses. That's how my life started, my different life," says Vanessa. She writhes around in skimpy dresses onstage, but offstage she is soft-spoken. A fellow performer, Diana, who is animated, with red-streaked hair, agrees. "It never starts as anything sexual, because as a kid that doesn't make sense. You just know you like girl things, and that you are different."

It was in the 70s, in New York City, that Teanga started transitioning—taking hormones. "Back then, you could do your transition and take hormones, but you still had to dress like a man. Only on the weekends could you be a woman—and this is in New York, not even Puerto Rico!"

Other things have changed, too. On a slow snowy night at La Cueva, two lesbian couples arrive just after midnight to cuddle at dark tables while gay men slow-dance under the disco ball. At the bar, there are a few solo Mexican cowboys. But in the 80s when the show started, it wasn't as LGBT friendly.

"Now it is all gay and lesbian. In my day, it was straight men who came," says Teanga, a little longingly. "I was seen as a woman, so straight men came." It sounds sort of progressive, but the transphobia was also much higher. "There were a lot of gangsters—they'd throw bottles and shoot at us with BB guns. You had to park your car and run inside," she says. According to the manager, Ruben Lechuga, the bar itself was feistier, with fewer bouncers and more fights.

Working at La Cueva makes the performers visible and therefore vulnerable. But the bar is one place offering Latina transwomen work—which can be hard to come by. "I've been working for La Cueva for nine years and I never before worked doing what I do now. I worked in other places like restaurants and temp office jobs. But I was frowned upon for applying with a male name but wanting to be a woman. They have issues with you going to the women's bathroom, things like that," Paula, a petite performer with chiseled features, says.

Of course, transphobia is not limited to Latina transwomen, but it can be more intense for them. Rodriguez says, "Transphobia has to an overwhelming degree curtailed the employment opportunities of transgender individuals. Latina transwomen, like African American transwomen, are also subject to racism. But when you add language to the mix, Latina transwomen may find it increasingly difficult to find work."

Regardless of the language barrier—which is significant, as the performers only speak Spanish—the United States is where these women can find jobs. "Before this, I worked out in the fields in Mexico, and I always dreamed about working in a place doing what I do now," Vanessa says. Diana explains it as feeling more safe. "I feel gays are more understood here." Mexico City may have legalized gay marriage, but Vanessa and Paula assert that homophobia within the community remains. It seems that as gay issues get press, this tension grows. "In Mexico they changed the law to where gay marriages are allowed, but they will still call you out on the street or yell dirty things, much worse than here," says Paula.

Rodriguez sees it as a larger problem. "While educating people on transgender lives is key, I also believe there must be a more concerted effort by queers and straight allies alike to advocate for rights and fair treatment for transgender people. Unfortunately middle-class, privileged issues like gay marriage continue to overshadow the blatant racial and economic discrepancies faced by those purportedly accounted for in the LGBT community," he says.

But in her 50 years of being out as transgender, Teanga has seen a change in the attitudes of the Latino community toward gays. "Latinos are just becoming more positive and proud of gays, but only somewhat of transgendered people."

Rodriguez agrees. "I'm inclined to say the Latino community has become more gay—accepting—but this suggests that Latinos have always been homophobic. This is not necessarily true. While Latino religious and cultural values often stand at odds with homosexuality, many Latino families have accepted LGBT members. We are witnessing more Latino LGBT media representations (Ricky Martin, for example) that are, fortunately, raising awareness and igniting conversation about homosexuality in the Latino community."

When I talk to the performers, the importance of their work comes back to community. "We are all Latinos here. You can make friends here, talk, and overall have a good time," Diana says. "This is a place that opens its doors to the Latino gay community as well as anyone."

Teanga pinpoints the moment when things began to change for her, and by extension for all trans performers. "So, the saxophone was playing. And I started to take off my clothes. And my body was curvy from the hormones. That is when the shows changed. It became about femme, not men in drag."

Dating with an STD
Lynn Harris

Susie Carrillo was 21 years old and a mother of two young children when an abnormal Pap smear yielded a triple-whammy nightmare. She was shocked not only by a diagnosis of high-grade cervical dysplasia—a serious precancerous condition—but also by its apparent cause: human papillomavirus (HPV), a sexually transmitted infection, or STI, more commonly known as STD, for sexually transmitted disease. A doctor had found it two years earlier but had largely dismissed it, saying, eh, it'll probably clear up on its own. With no warnings about the risks of cancer, or transmission, Carrillo says she "just didn't think about it" and told no one. And that's what led, in part, to the third and perhaps biggest whammy of all: her husband's reaction to the cause of her cancer. "He turned it into hell for me. He demanded to know how many people I'd slept with, accused me of cheating, and called me a slut," she says. Even though Carrillo had never strayed—she believes she contracted HPV from a premarriage ex—her husband's abusive words began to infect her, too. "I started to wonder if maybe it *was* my fault," she says. Ashamed and embarrassed, she went through cancer treatment alone.

Thankfully, Carrillo was eventually cured: of both her cancer and her self-blame. She ultimately divorced her husband, found support online, and learned, as she says, that she has "nothing to be ashamed about." But even with its happy ending, her story reveals a troubling reality: While STIs have reached pandemic proportions, the stigma surrounding them remains ugly—perhaps especially for women.

"You cannot get through a season of *Jersey Shore* or *The Real World* without an STI joke implying that the person accused of having one is skanky and slutty, and saying 'Ooh, watch out, you might catch something,'" says Adina Nack PhD, a medical sociologist specializing in sexual health and author of *Damaged Goods? Women Living with Incurable Sexually Transmitted Diseases*. "And that person they're talking about is almost always a woman. There's a serious misconception that you have to be promiscuous in order to contract an STI, and while men in our culture are rewarded for being sexually active, women are judged." (Nack cites one woman in her practice who'd never even had sex, but who contracted an STI while—successfully—fighting off a rapist. Even she said, "I feel like a slut.")

To be sure, STIs and their attendant stigmas are (as I've written elsewhere) no picnic for men, either. But their impact appears to be different, in certain ways, for women. Among the hundreds of people with STIs Nack has interviewed, she says, men tend to be more concerned about medical realities—the best treatment, the best protection for partners—while women focus on much broader, and harsher, implications that strike at the very core of their sexual selves: "Will I be rejected as 'damaged goods'?" "Are my dreams for sex, love and happiness over?"

This is ironic, considering that STIs are now so strikingly common that, as Nack says, "you should go out into the dating world assuming that the person you're with has already contracted something, even though they may not know it. Even if someone says, 'I'm clean—I've been tested for everything,' they're either ignorant or lying, because we don't even have definitive tests for everything." STIs are often asymptomatic and frequently go undiagnosed. The CDC estimates that nearly 19 million new infections occur each year. At least *half* of the sexually active population will contract HPV at some point; 45 percent of women 20 to 24 have it already. It's so prevalent, in fact, that the medical community considers HPV infection a virtual marker for having had sex at all. One in five adults, whether they know it or not, has herpes right now. In other words, statistically, your date is more likely to carry a sexually transmitted infection than to share your astrological sign.

Though many STIs are easily and effectively treatable, those who have them still live with threats: of painful outbreaks, other medical complications and (in the case of certain HPV strains) cervical cancer; of straight-up slut-shaming and outright rejection. Given how common STIs are—and despite efforts by, for example, writers at the blog Jezebel to chip away at the stigma by indirectly or directly outing themselves—it's pretty amazing how much dated stereotype and outright ignorance remains, which in turn can deter people from getting tested. People whom both Nack and I interviewed tell tales of women with herpes who, when actually outed, were told by officemates to use separate work equipment, and by family members to use separate toilets.

And if people you're probably not going to sleep with react

badly, imagine having to tell someone you *like*-like. For single women (and of course men) with STIs, the fizzy fun of a promising new date is often flattened, they say, by fear of the looming, dreaded Talk. Michele Bouffidis, 43, of New Jersey, contracted herpes—her "rowdy tenant," she calls it, though she experiences only rare outbreaks—from an old long-term boyfriend who didn't tell her he had it until it was too late. Over the next five years, she dared disclose to three men; none stuck around. One, at least, took the time to consider, eventually telling her—gently and thoughtfully—that he didn't want to take the risk. She totally understood, she says, but it still smarted. Another said, "You seem like a very classy girl—I would never have imagined *you* having *that*." (Translation: "You slut.") By the time No. 3 rolled around, Bouffidis was dispirited enough that she presented her diagnosis in a negative, "You're not going to want to deal with this," light, almost deliberately pushing him away. For three years, she didn't date at all. "It *was* because I have herpes," she confirms. "I didn't want to deal with the Talk anymore."

Kalani Tom, 40, of New York, usually uses email to inform potential partners about her genital herpes (which she controls successfully with medication) to give them a chance to process the information on their own. Sometimes, it goes fine. "One guy said, 'It's gonna take a lot more than that to scare me off,'" she recalls. But the more she likes a guy, the scarier it is—and once, when the stakes were high, she choked. "He asked me if I had anything, and I said no," she admits. "I was a coward. I didn't want to be judged." When she finally told him the truth, he was devastated—not just by her diagnosis, but by her dishonesty. (Fortunately, he tested negative.) Another recent prospect just bailed, too, upon hearing the news. But Tom—though quite contrite about her lie—remains hopeful, even defiant. "People may judge, but I know I'm not some repulsive horrible person," she says.

Plenty of STI-seropositive men and women—Nack herself included (and Michele, above)—are in happy, healthy relationships with STI-free partners willing to take on the medical logistics of avoiding transmission. "Not all potential partners are going to reject you," she says. And many women and men with STIs have found support, community, friends—and more than friends—in online communities specifically for them. There's an interesting, and ongoing, debate about whether dating sites for people with STIs are godsends or ghettos, but experts say they are—at least— great places for the newly diagnosed to get their groove back.

Kristin Andrews, 30, of Michigan, contracted herpes from an unfaithful boyfriend who, when he heard her diagnosis, called her "a slut and a whore and complained that now it's gonna be hard for *him* to date," she recalls. "For that first few weeks it was awful. I felt like I was one of the worst people in the world, disgusting and degraded and gross." Then she found MPwH.net (short for Meet People with Herpes), where she got her "newbie" questions answered straightforwardly and reassuringly. Eventually, she arrived at the distinction that our society clearly—and dangerously—still refuses to accept: "I have herpes," she says. "But it's not who I am."

You Can Have Sex with Them; Just Don't Photograph Them

Radley Balko

In spring and summer 2006, Eric Rinehart, at the time a 34-year-old police officer in the small town of Middletown, Indiana, began consensual sexual relationships with two young women, ages 16 and 17. One of the women had contacted Rinehart through his MySpace page. He had known the other one, the daughter of a man who was involved in training police officers, for most of her life. Rinehart was going through a divorce at the time. The relationships came to the attention of local authorities, and then federal authorities, when one of the girls mentioned it to a guidance counselor.

Whatever you might think of Rinehart's judgment or ethics, his relationships with the girls weren't illegal. The age of consent in Indiana is 16. That is also the age of consent in federal territories. Rinehart got into legal trouble because one of the girls mentioned to him that she had posed for sexually provocative photos for a previous boyfriend and offered to do the same for Rinehart. Rinehart lent her his camera, which she returned with the promised photos. Rinehart and both girls then took additional photos and at least one video, which he downloaded to his computer.

In 2007, Rinehart was convicted on two federal charges of producing child pornography. US District Court Judge David Hamilton, who now serves on the US Court of Appeals for the 7th Circuit, reluctantly sentenced Rinehart to 15 years in prison. Thanks to mandatory minimum sentences, Hamilton wrote, his hands were tied. There is no parole in the federal prison system. So barring an unlikely grant of clemency from the president, Rinehart, who is serving his time at a medium-security prison in Pennsylvania, will have to complete at least 85 percent of his term (assuming time off for good behavior), or nearly 13 years.

Hamilton was not permitted to consider any mitigating factors in sentencing Rinehart. It did not matter that Rinehart's sexual relationships with the two girls were legal. Nor did it matter that the photos for which he was convicted never went beyond his computer. Rinehart had no prior criminal history, and there was no evidence he had ever possessed or searched for child pornography on his computer. There was also no evidence that he abused his position as a police officer to lure the two women into sex. His crime was producing for his own use explicit images of two physically mature women with whom he was legally having sex. (Both women also could have legally married Rinehart without their parents' consent, although it's unclear whether federal law would have permitted a prosecution of Rinehart for photographing his own wife.)

"You can certainly conceive of acts of producing actual child pornography, the kind that does real harm to children, for which a fifteen-year sentence would be appropriate," says Mary Price, general counsel for the criminal justice reform group Families Against Mandatory Minimums. "But this is a single-factor trigger, so it gets applied in cases like this one, where the sentence really doesn't fit the culpability."

In his sentencing statement, Hamilton urges executive clemency for Rinehart. He points out that under federal law Rinehart received the same sentence someone convicted of hijacking an airplane or second-degree murder would receive. For a bank robber to get Rinehart's sentence, Hamilton writes, "he would need to fire a gun, inflict serious bodily injury on a victim, physically restrain another victim, and get away with the stunning total of $2.5 million." (You might also compare Rinehart's punishment to the treatment given former Elkhart, Indiana, police officer William Lee. Lee, who had a history of "inappropriately touching" women while on the job, was recently fired for using the threat of an arrest warrant to coerce a woman into having sex with him. He was never criminally charged.)

Hamilton is not the first federal judge to express frustration over federal child porn sentencing laws. In May 2010, *the New York Times* profiled US District Court Judge Jack Weinstein, who after 43 years on the bench has essentially gone rogue, twice throwing out convictions of a man convicted of receiving child pornography because of the five-year mandatory minimum sentence attached to the offense. Weinstein has also indicated that in future child porn cases he will disregard the federal rules of criminal procedure and inform his juries of the sentences defendants will get if convicted.

Rinehart was convicted of producing child pornography. But in cases where a suspect is charged with receiving child pornography, prosecutors need not even show intent. The mere presence of the images on the defendant's computer is enough to win a conviction. "Each image can be a separate count, so these sentences can add up pretty quickly," Price says. "And with a video, each frame can count as a separate image. So if you accidentally or unknowingly download a video that's later discovered on your computer, you could be looking at a really long sentence."

In a 2010 survey by the US Sentencing Commission, 71 percent of the 585 federal judges who responded thought the five-year mandatory minimum for receiving child pornography was too harsh. Just 2 percent thought it was too lenient. Only the mandatory minimum for crack cocaine, which has since been reduced, met with wider disapproval.

"When judges don't abide by sentencing guidelines, the logical conclusion would be that the guidelines are flawed, that they should be revised to better reflect culpability," Price says. "Instead, the reaction from Congress is too often to make the guidelines mandatory, or to make the sentences even harsher."

It could actually have been worse for Rinehart. Under federal law, he could have faced up to 25 years in prison. In exchange for a guilty plea, prosecutors agreed to seek only the minimum sentence. Unfortunately for Rinehart, that plea agreement also prevents him from challenging his conviction or sentence. His only hope for early release is executive clemency. Given the clemency records of the last two administrations, that does not seem likely.

Rinehart's case also illustrates the advantages of federalism. Traditionally, criminal law has been left to the states. Age of consent in particular is an issue that is best decided at the state or local level, where lawmakers can set boundaries that reflect local values. The 1984 federal law that Rinehart was charged with breaking, which raised the federal age of consent for explicit images from 16 to 18, was passed under the authority of the Commerce Clause. According to the prevailing interpretation of the clause, the federal government has a legitimate interest in regulating the interstate sale and distribution of child pornography (by prohibiting it) to prevent the exploitation of children.

But the women Rinehart photographed were not children. Under Indiana (and federal) law, they were adults. Furthermore, Rinehart not only was not a producer of actual child pornography; he was not even a consumer. His decision to photograph and upload to his computer photos and video of the two women had no effect whatsoever on the interstate market for child pornography.

You could argue that it makes sense to have a higher age of consent for sexually explicit photos than for sexual activity because photos can be preserved and distributed. That means one bad decision can cause lasting harm, something a 16- or 17-year-old disoriented by love or passion may not be mature enough to consider.

But as Hamilton points out in his sentencing statement, there is no indication that Congress had this rationale in mind when it raised the age of consent in 1984. Instead the congressional record indicates the reason for the change was that prosecutors usually are not able to track down the women depicted in explicit photos to verify their ages. With the cutoff at 16, prosecutors were having problems winning convictions if the girls depicted in the images showed any signs of puberty. Raising the age to 18, a House committee reported, "would facilitate the prosecution of child pornography cases and raise the effective age of protection of children from these practices probably not to 18 years of age, but perhaps to 16."

In Rinehart's case, however, there is no question about the age or identity of the "victims." So why did Assistant US Attorney Steven DeBrota—who has won awards for his efforts to break up actual child pornography rings—decide to turn Rinehart's questionable judgment into a federal felony?

"This seemed like it was all going to be sorted out locally," says Stacy Rinehart, Eric Rinehart's sister. "They had a deal worked out where they were going to charge Eric for some sort of misconduct, and he'd do time in a local jail away from other inmates. Police officers don't tend to do very well in prison. But then the FBI got involved. And no one really knows why. I can only guess it was because Eric was a police officer when all this happened, and maybe they thought that made what he did worse. But he had a good record, and they never put on any evidence that he abused his position."

DeBrota didn't return my call requesting comment. But the fact that a federal prosecutor would pursue a case like this one demonstrates the problem of taking sentencing discretion away from judges. It is true that, technically, Rinehart violated federal law. But no reasonable person would call him a child pornographer, and it seems unlikely that Congress was thinking of people like him when they raised the federal age of consent for sexually explicit images. Putting him away for 15 years hardly feels like justice.

An Unfortunate Discharge Early in My Naval Career

Tim Elhajj

My first year in the United States Navy, I let another boy give me a blow job simply because he asked. Of course we were caught. If we hadn't been caught, this wouldn't be a story. I probably wouldn't even remember the night in question. This was in San Diego, over 30 years ago, and we had been drinking. As far as oral sex goes, it was disappointing. He was young and inexperienced: a quiet, doe-eyed boy, big as an ox.

We had met earlier that year at a naval training facility in Connecticut, just before receiving our fleet assignments. I didn't like him, but I didn't dislike him either. I knew his name was Fear. In the military everyone goes by their last names. I don't even remember his first. When we parted ways in Connecticut, I had no idea we'd meet again. After training, he had gone on to the fleet, while I was temporarily assigned to a recruiting office near my hometown, a small mill town in Pennsylvania. I was sup-

posed to visit the local high schools in my dress whites, a choice
duty they probably only gave me because I was 17. My mother
had to sign papers so I could enlist.

But I never appeared at a single high school event that summer.
I'd like to say this was because I didn't want to be used as a tool
for the man, but the truth is, I was scared. The thought of talking
to a room full of students terrified me. I had been thrown out of
high school three times: twice in my junior year, and then again
as a senior. Chief among my problems was the knee-jerk way in
which I responded to authority, though I would not have been
able to describe it this way at that time. Even if I couldn't articu-
late my problems, I knew I was deficient in ways that most students were not. I also understood that most adults—particularly
the recruiting officers who were now my peers—did not suspect
how lacking I was. I couldn't bring myself to visit any of the
school events the recruiters had organized, because I felt certain
the students would see right through me, past my crisp starched
creases and glossy black shoes to the little boy hiding inside. So
I stuck with my own hometown crowd who were celebrating
the onset of summer, or their own high school graduations, by
shooting heroin instead.

I joined the fleet late in August.

Flying into San Diego, I knew I had missed movement of my
newly assigned ship, a serious offense in its own right. But I wasn't
too concerned: I had come up with a pretty convincing lie. On
the tender, a yeoman first class named Thompson took my packet
of orders. He shuffled through the paperwork and said he thought
I might have missed my ship's movement. I launched into my in-
nocent-boy routine—the surprised gasp, the agonized wringing
of hands. I offered my story and then paced the tiny space, my
forehead growing moist. I had only been chipping heroin, but de-

spite these nominal amounts, I found myself irritable and restless, which I'm sure only added to the illusion I was trying to convey. Thompson did just as I hoped he would: in a commanding voice he told me to relax. To sit down. He would take it from here. Thompson was the yeoman for the Pacific Seaboard's entire submarine fleet. I felt pleased that my little ploy had gotten the better of him, but it would cost me dearly in the months to come.

I eventually got a room in the barracks and waited for new orders.

In the base cafeteria, I ran into Quish, another sailor I knew from Connecticut. He had thin, dark hair, with a thick white strip that hung in his eyes. He was stationed on a boat out of Hawaii but was in San Diego for training. He seemed pleased to see me, and in his thick Boston accent invited me over to his room to drink. I readily agreed. As an afterthought, he mentioned that Fear was on his boat and in San Diego for the same training.

"You remember Fear?" he asked.

I shrugged. I had a vague idea who he might be.

Quish considered this for a second or two. His barrel chest heaved as he inhaled through his mouth, the way big men sometimes do. "Come by tonight," he said. "Maybe you'll remember when you see him."

Later that night, I sat alone in a small office.

After pounding on my door at 4:00 a.m., a pair of burly MPs brought me here, a small building in an unfamiliar part of the base. We drove over in a dark sedan, the MPs quietly murmuring in the front, me in the back. The sky was dark, the cool air thick with the smell of the sea.

I heard people in the rooms outside the tiny office, but the blind on the door window was drawn, and I couldn't see who was out there or how many there were. The metal desk in front of me had file folders and forms strewn across it. There was a torch lamp. Stacks of thick dark-blue binders were piled along one side of the room.

The pain in my back had mostly subsided, but to keep from aggravating my sore body, I sat up in my seat and waited for whatever would happen next. Although I was in the thick of trouble, I felt weirdly calm, which I couldn't explain. I felt as if I were watching a story unfold, even though I knew this was my story, and these events were happening to me.

In walked two men in rumpled dark suits and thin, loosened neckties. The stocky one sat behind the desk and introduced himself as an agent of the naval investigative service, which he told me was the NIS. He flashed an identification card and badge from a little leather holder. His partner unbuttoned his jacket and leaned against a file cabinet. He held a paper cup of coffee in his hand.

I had a terrible taste in my mouth from drinking earlier that evening, but I didn't feel the least bit intoxicated now. In fact, my mind seemed to be in some hyperaware, vigilant place. I was thinking how strange it was that I felt so composed when I noticed that my knee was working itself like a piston. I willed my knee to stop, to match the calm exterior I wanted to present.

"Did you visit the *Sperry*'s infirmary earlier tonight?" The agent behind the desk asked. The USS *Sperry* was the tender moored to the pier. He held some paperwork that I realized was probably from the doctors on the tender.

"I did," I said. No point lying here.

"Why?" he wanted to know.

"I got into a fight," I said.

"With who?"

"A guy in the barracks named Quish," I said. I went over all this with the doctors, so I was sure it was in his report. What wasn't in his report was this: Right after the fight with Quish, I had raced to the *Sperry*. Not because I was hurt—although I did get the worst of the fight—but to try to weasel out of the mess that I knew was about to go hot. My goal was to get something in writing that offered me some plausible deniability. Quish was to be my main opponent, and this time I wanted to put up a better fight.

"Why were you fighting?" the agent asked.

My voice stuck: this was the $64,000 dollar question.

"You should ask Quish," I said. "He started it." This was true.

Quish had hammered with his fists on my barracks door. I wanted to go out there and calm him down. Play it off like he was drunk. Like he had certainly not seen what he thought he'd seen. But there is something about witnessing an act of homosexuality that so wounds and incenses a certain type of man, he cannot be reasoned with. And if he cannot be reasoned with, you should certainly not attempt to lie to him. But I didn't realize any of this at the time. I opened the barracks door to boldly assert my innocence and Quish promptly bowled me over. I would have taken a beating, but Fear came out of the closet (literally) and saved my ass.

Watching those two titans crash around the room was like watching one of those old Japanese monster movies from the 60s. For such a quiet boy, Fear knew how to defend himself. Quish soon retreated to his end of the hall, screaming, "Faggots! Goddamn, fucking faggots!"

"Why do you think you were fighting?" the agent asked.

The doctors on the *Sperry* had not pressed this issue. This was my first inkling that things had escalated, gone from bad to worse. This was no more than six hours after Quish saw Fear and me through the barracks window, and the barracks fight that followed.

"He was drunk," I said. "We had been drinking."

A big sigh from the agent leaning on the cabinet. "Show him," the agent said to his partner. He straightened and sipped his coffee.

"Just show him," he repeated.

"Hold on," the seated agent said. He sounded annoyed. He cocked his head toward his partner, holding out his hands palm up. "I got this. I got it."

Placing his hands on the desk in front of him, the seated agent leaned forward.

"You," he said to me, "are a homosexual." He paused here for a beat. "And we do not allow homosexuals in the United States Navy."

I was shocked at his blunt accusation.

I didn't think of myself as a homosexual, even though this was not the first time I had had sex with a man. I didn't even use the word *homosexual*. I said *faggot*, or maybe *queer*. If I was trying to be diplomatic, I might have said *homo* or *fag*.

When I was in high school, I hustled gay men, even though I knew there were more lucrative ways to make money—ways that didn't come at such a high emotional cost. If I'd stolen hubcaps or engaged in an afternoon of shoplifting, I wouldn't have spent endless hours agonizing over what those behaviors really meant about me. As an adult, I realize that I continued to hustle because I liked the attention, the power, and the money. But I especially liked to be prized by men, probably because I longed to bond with the men in my family—my father and older brothers—and rarely succeeded.

When my boyhood friend—let's call him Smack—first suggested hustling, he did so by taking me aside and asking if I'd ever had a blow job. Yes, I lied immediately, even as I felt the blood rushing to my face. We were in the apartment of a man who distributed bundles of the local afternoon paper from the back of his Ford station wagon. He was in the back room, a balding man, with a greasy wisp of a ponytail and a mouth filled with twisted teeth. Smack saw through my lie and started to snicker. I assured him that, yes, I had, even as I grew embarrassed by the whiny tone of my voice. Smack swallowed his laugh and whispered, "Homos give the best head." I loved the low conspiratorial tone of his voice, loved the idea of receiving a secret from him, of being in his confidence. He had already quit school. He was good with his fists and one of the first to walk around our small town with his shirt off at the start of May—ribs, bony shoulders, and curly brown crown. Without naming any names, Smack assured me that this was what everyone did. I felt my determination wane. *Homos give the best head.*

I named a mutual friend—Smack solemnly nodded—and then I named another. He leaned toward me, brought his lips to my ear. "Everyone," he whispered.

This turned out to be a lie. Smack and I were the only ones hustling gay men.

Before I agreed to go into the room with the paper delivery man, I wanted to ask Smack what it might mean for me to have sex with another man, especially if I wasn't—I would have stumbled over what word to use here, and *queer* is probably the word I'd have settled on, had I been able to ask the question. But I couldn't. I couldn't figure out how to pose the question. Instead, I asked Smack about the paper delivery man's mangled teeth. Would it hurt, I wanted to know.

Smack just chuckled.

The agents were talking to me, but I wasn't paying attention. Looking down, I noticed my right leg pistoning again, but this time I didn't attempt to make it stop.

"I'm not homosexual." I had to choke out this word. "I'm not."

I blurted this out and the agent sitting at the desk stopped talking. The man standing chuckled and tossed his coffee into the trash, cup and all.

"Quish says he saw you having sex with…" The agent looked into the folder in front of him. "Fear," he said.

"That's a lie," I said. I spoke with confidence. Of course, I was lying here, purposely ignoring the act. My confidence was born of the only thing of which I felt certain that night: I was no queer.

"Quish is lying," I said.

The agent sat back in his chair and sighed.

"What does Fear say?" I asked.

I felt certain Fear would back me up. With Fear and me against Quish, we were certain to win. The agents exchanged a glance. Seeing this look pass between them, I felt emboldened. "Get Fear in here," I said. "He'll straighten this out."

"Fear's gone," the agent said.

I leaned back in my seat, confused.

The agent looked at his watch. "Right now Fear is about halfway to…" He leaned forward and checked the paperwork. "Michigan," he said.

"Holy shit," I said.

"We do not allow homosexuals in the United States Navy," the agent standing said. "Fear was a homosexual."

"You," the seated agent said, "are a homosexual."

"No," I said, although even I knew I didn't sound too convincing.

The agent at the desk tugged out a sheaf of handwritten paper on a yellow legal pad and passed it over to me. When I asked what it was, he told me that Fear had written a statement. I saw the big loops of Fear's penmanship, neat and precise. I knew the agents were watching me. I shuffled through the pages but I didn't bother to read the words. I wondered what I would tell the people back home. I felt a sort of sick awareness growing in my gut. I thought about facing my father, my brothers. I thought about Smack, who would probably laugh at me. I had intended to use the military to turn my life around but had always imagined that the change of course—the about-face—would happen in due time, that it would simply overtake me and somehow sweep me off my feet.

"It's a lie," I said.

I hadn't really understood the stakes earlier, but now I was terrified, blinking to keep back the tears. I joined the Navy to become a man. This thought seemed so ridiculous that I made an unbidden snort, even as I fought to stay in control of myself. I had no way of knowing that I was about to take my first few tentative steps toward manhood. I was about to be forced to tear off the mask I had worn through high school. About to stand revealed before the adult world and acknowledge who I really was: a heterosexual male who struggled with authority, an indiscriminate rebel who had a weakness for a little good head.

I exhaled noisily.

I realized the agents were waiting for me to speak. I supposed they wanted me to say that I was homosexual. And then I realized that I was thousands of miles away from everyone I knew, my entire family and all my friends, in a land filled with strangers. I was sitting with two NIS agents who thought they had my number. I looked at the agent standing by the file cabinet, the agent sitting behind the desk. I had always imagined it would be a therapist who suggested that deep down I was gay. These agents didn't look half qualified. On whose authority could they tell me what I am? When I thought of it in terms of authority, the decision was easier to see. I could feel my blood rising. All in a rush, I came to the usual conclusion: *No*, I thought.

Fuck you.

I took a deep breath, my eyes narrowed.

Earlier in the week, I had been watching afternoon TV in the lobby of the barracks. One of those old detective shows from the 70s was on—*Cannon*, maybe? *Colombo*? The detective confronted a criminal with a sheaf of paperwork. The criminal looked at it and threw it to the floor. "Dis reads like a comic book," he said.

I tossed Fear's statement onto the desk and glared at the agents. "This reads like a comic book," I said, trying to scowl convincingly.

Together both agents sighed as one.

They told me that I had just chosen to do it the hard way. This was true, for it was 1979: long before "Don't ask, don't tell," or the current swell of popular support for allowing gays and lesbians to serve in the armed forces. I would discover that it took the better part of a year to sort this out. During that time, I would find some champions, in particular a young lieutenant junior grade who would help me get a lawyer and deal with some logistical issues. But I had already made some powerful enemies— Thompson and Quish—and I would make a few more before the year was through. As I awaited the outcome of my military tribunal, my father would grow suddenly ill, waste away, and die. By then he had discovered that I was using heroin on my visits home, and he wanted to discuss it with me. Because the stigma of heroin addiction was less damaging than the stigma of having sex with another man, I would shame myself in the last days of his life by resolving that, even if captain's mast went badly, at least Dad would never know what happened to me in the Navy.

To cope with my father's death, my mother and most of my siblings would cloak themselves in the mantle of fundamentalist Christianity that swept the nation at the time. On emergency leave visits that winter, I would think of Anita Bryant and her ongoing campaign against homosexuality. *You can't go home again.*

It would be years before I stopped using drugs, even longer before I came to some understanding about my sexuality. But from this experience I learned what it felt like to be an outcast, to come face to face with my fears about the kind of man God made me to be. I would eventually be allowed to remain in the Navy, but the submarine base in San Diego was a small community, and as in all small communities, word traveled fast. On any given day, half the base wanted to kick my ass—while more than a few of the rest wanted to blow me.

Summertime in San Diego, lying in my bed in the cool of the night. Hearing a knock on my barracks door, I would get up and reach for the doorknob, never really knowing which way it would go—proposition or fistfight—until I came out into the hallway light.

Guys Who Like Fat Chicks

Camille Dodero

Dan Weiss is 26, stands five foot six, weighs about 130 pounds, and has a thin chinstrap beard outlining his jaw—without the scruff, he looks 12. This Tuesday afternoon in March is the first time we've ever met, even though he's a freelance music writer and we've been emailing each other professionally for years.

I first took an interest in him in September 2009, when he reviewed a live show of the Coathangers, a scrappy all-female grrrl-wave four-piece group from Atlanta. In a note that was apropos of nothing really, he mentioned that he had taken out a description of the women in the band as "super-cute," because, he said, he didn't want anyone to think he was into "skinny girls."

His Facebook profile filled in some of the blanks. He wore black-rimmed glasses and uniformly tight band T-shirts. He had shaggy black hair that fell in wiry squiggles. He played guitar and studied English at William Paterson University. There were snapshots of him posed with a beautiful young woman who appeared to be more than twice his size, wearing a French-maid Halloween costume. And there was a link to *Ask a Guy Who Likes Fat Chicks*, an unsigned advice-column blog "for your plumper-related stumpers."

Blog entries happily, ravenously, referenced double bellies, back rolls, and "big old ham thighs." Feminine body shapes were compared to pears, apples, and in one case, a calabash squash; their weights spanned from 180 pounds to over 500. "Big Fat Sexy Kitty," a young woman who described herself as five feet tall and 260 pounds, wrote in: "I want fat sex. I want my jiggly bits rubbed and squished and fondled sexually."

In person at the East Village's Cafe Orlin, Dan explains that, yes, he likes round bellies. He likes double chins. He likes breasts the size of his head. He loves flabby biceps. "Fat upper arms are awesome. I would almost say I'm an arms guy," he says, not by any means whispering. "I didn't know that they would be that soft. I, like, fell asleep on a girl's arm once. I was like, 'Wow.'"

The *Ask a Guy Who Likes Fat Chicks* blog began on a whim, with Dan posting during his border-crossing bus sojourns to visit his long-distance girlfriend of two years, the smoky-eyed French maid from Toronto. The phrase "fat chicks" was meant to be a reversal of the college-humor slogan "No fat chicks." And in the online world of Facebook groups and BBW (Big Beautiful Woman) message boards that Dan inhabits, "fat" is preferable to "overweight," which implies a standard, or "hefty," which belongs to the trash bag, or "heavy," which sounds like furniture. And "fat admirer" is the most frequent shorthand for straight men who prefer fat partners—the better-known term "chubby chaser" has become associated with the gay community.

Too lazy to consider himself an activist, but cocky enough to be the mouthy weakling "who would be getting my neck rung by the bully and still saying shit," Dan is ego-driven enough to envision a greater purpose. "Society sucks, and society says you need male validation. If you're trying to say fat is attractive, as a lot of women out there are, it helps to find legitimate people who find this attractive." Or, as he put it more bluntly on his Facebook page, after contributing two pro-fat pieces to lady blog *The Hairpin*, "I write about my preference for fat women in hopes that other men who share my preference will make themselves known so they'll stop being little ballsacks and let the millions of fat women in this country find them."

In other words, Guys Who Like Fat Chicks are not make-believe. "We're out there."

Dear Askaguywholikesfatchicks:
Why do you like fat chicks?
—Sincerely, A Fat Chick

I'm so glad you asked. But the answer is: I don't know. It's the same I-don't-know that pubescent boys will tell you after waking up strangely soaked from a night of dreaming about—I don't know, Ashley Tisdale. The real question is, why are so many Fat Admirers in denial? I can't tell you how many guys (or gals) there are like me, and a good portion of them being in the closet makes the numbers even fuzzier. Over half the US population is considered—DUN-DUN-DUN—"overweight." Someone's fucking all the fatties.* Be a sport and let them know.

*Contrary to popular belief, it's not me. [January 7, 2009]

Once upon a time, if a young man wanted to see a fat girl naked, he actually had to woo her. *Playboy* and *Penthouse* didn't publish stretch-mark-mapped centerfolds. BBW nude-model paysites like PlumpPrincess.com and BigCuties.com did not exist. Dan Weiss didn't have that problem. "An early memory was having *Entertainment Weekly*, cutting out pictures of Anna Nicole Smith in the Guess ads, and just studying her boobs," he says. But unlike his fat-appreciating forebears, he had the Internet. "I was looking for bigger and bigger boobs online, and when you looked at bigger and bigger boobs, you wound up finding bigger girls. And I was like, *Oh, wait. I like all of this.*"

Kevin N., a marine biology doctoral candidate at the University of Maine, Orono, figured it out on the school bus in high school. "This girl sat next to me, and she was about three hundred pounds—she was gorgeous, she was blond," he tells me over the phone. "That day, everyone had to sit three to a seat. I was up against the window, she had to push up against me, and the other kid was sitting with one ass cheek hanging off the seat. I'm just sitting there with my backpack on my lap, like, Hunhhhh." That was the first public erection he ever had. "You realize, *I think I like this.*"

Immediately, that made Kevin different. "In high school, you have your prototypical locker-room discussion, 'Hey, did you see so-and-so?'" he says. "You can't come out and say, 'Oh, no, not really,' because then you'll get, 'What are you, some sort of fag?'"

That's what everyone assumed about the Red Sox fan anyway. A basketball player with type 1 diabetes, Kevin was five foot ten and 131 pounds at his Coventry, Rhode Island high school. Meanwhile, his "pretty" girlfriend was an all-state softball player—size 16, five feet nine inches tall, maybe 200 pounds—but she could bench more than her scrawny boyfriend. A rumor spread that he was gay, which he didn't bother to refute. Liking a fat girl was so much more preposterous that he worried the truth would "make it snowball even more." Kevin recently became engaged to a 25-year-old Ohio woman he met five years ago in a BBW chat room.

Fat Admirers (FA) have historically adopted queer nomenclature for their self-discovery stages and preferences. Men who openly pursue, prefer, and date fat women are "out." Men who like fat women but more or less hide them from friends and family are "closeted." Men who say they like both skinny and supersize women are "bisizuals," a controversial term that's regarded as disingenuous in various online circles.

Keith Ferguson, a 24-year-old FA from Westchester ("We had two African American kids in our schools and one fat girl"), wonders if he would have been treated better if he'd been gay. "The immediate reception from my friends was, 'You're a fetishistic freak, and I can't believe I hang out with you.'" He confided in a friend who then spilled it to their freshman class. "It's almost like the same level of stigma that a homosexual would deal with. But in high school, there were two 'out' gay kids before I turned 16. People were like, 'Ah-hahaha, you're gay.' They were maybe on the outskirts of the socially accepted circle, at the end of the day, but enough people liked them that it didn't really matter. For me, I was actually ostracized."

Even from his family. Keith, a six-foot-one, 180-pound blond smoker who was raised eating "twigs and sticks," didn't speak to his mother for years. "She always had a certain mentality. She'd make jokes like, 'If I got that fat, just smack me.' *The Biggest Loser* is her favorite show: she's like, 'Oh, my God, I can't believe how much weight they lost.' She's obsessed with not being fat." There were other problems at home, but Keith's declaration, at age 12, that he liked fat chicks was the tipping point. "For her son to prefer fat women? That was her biggest nightmare in the world," he says. He moved out by the time he was 15.

"If someone starts talking about guys who like fat women or girls who like fat men, the first reaction is, 'Ewww,'" Keith says. He lovingly rubs the tummy of his 300-pound 30-something professor girlfriend in a corner booth at the Nolita bar Puck Fair. ("I'm the only fat person in my building, by far," she admits. "I walk around this area and I never see fat people.") Keith continues, "The second reaction is, 'What the fuck is wrong with you?' The third is, 'That is so unhealthy, and you're killing the person you want to be with.' It all leads up to: 'We don't want to talk to you. Get the fuck away.'"

> Dear Askaguywholikesfatchicks:
> Is it because fat girls are easy?
> —AAA
> If only. Try convincing an archetypal "easy" fat girl to do it with the light on, or let you play with her belly, or refer to her as "fat" without her sobbing and trying to throw up the nice dinner you bought her. Spend weeks convincing her you're Not Joking, your buddy's not gonna jump out of the closet with Tucker Max and a camera. Fat girls are just as complicated and frustrating as any other earthling.

The scoop on Lawrence (not his real name) is that he's charming, "impossibly smart," and a "bachelor," as Dan describes him—he dates, but he's keeping his options open. The 28-year-old Upper West Side resident says, "Ninety-nine percent of the women you see in magazines, I couldn't get it up for." He reluctantly adopts the Fat Admirer identifier, though he winces at the self-help sound of that moniker. "Fat Admirer? Do I ever really say that? I just like fat chicks, that's all.

"A girl you're in the office with will be like, 'I'm so fat, I'm never going to find anyone,'" he offers. "I will say, 'No, plenty of guys like that—it's not a negative, it's a positive.' And these women just"—he shakes his head in bemused disbelief—"vehemently deny it: 'Whatever, no, that's absolutely not true.' And it absolutely is." He hesitates. "I could go the next step and reveal myself," he admits. "But I don't want to talk about that at the office."

Fortunately, we're a safe distance away from the Theater District, where Lawrence holds a desk job in the "fairly gossipy" performing-arts field and aspires to become a producer. His professional ambitions are one reason the California native asked to be identified under a pseudonym. Another, he explains from the back corner of Malachy's Pub, a narrow West 72nd drinking trough, is the insidiously growing tentacles of the information era. "I don't want to be the guy who talks to a reporter about anything. It doesn't matter if it's fat chicks or sports or having peanut butter shoved up my ass." Peanut butter, you say? "I don't want sexuality to be on my public dossier."

Lawrence has thick brown hair, a beard that grows like crabgrass, and a toothy smile. He speaks confidently over whiskey, and as he lays out the popular misconceptions of "quote-unquote" Fat Admirers, it's with the measured air of someone delivering a prepared monologue.

Misconception #1: Loving fat women is a fetish.

"Steve, over there, has a type," says Lawrence, gesturing wanly at a stranger in a hockey jersey probably not named Steve. "I have a type, too. Mine's just bigger. He may like skinny blondes with bangs and long legs. I like pear shapes with brown hair and green eyes. I have a type—it just happens to be fat." Besides, people aren't fetish objects, they're people. "It's not like having a thing for leather."

Misconception #2: Fat Admirers pursue fat women because they are vulnerable prey.

"People seem to think we're like, 'I'm going to go after the weak zebra in the herd, the one that's limping along sad and pathetically in the back, and I'm going to exert one-third of the energy to get what I need.' First of all—" Lawrence hesitates awhile. "I was going to say that it's not easier for guys. That's a lie. It is." It's a fact that there's less competition. "That's unfortunate. But that has nothing to do with the impetus or the attraction."

Misconception #3: Guys who are sexually attracted to fat chicks are sexually attracted to all fat chicks.

"People often conflate bigness with beauty—being big is not what makes you beautiful, it's being both simultaneously," says Lawrence. "All the other normal benchmarks of attractiveness are in place. Proportions, symmetry, everything else, from tone of voice to texture of skin. That is exactly the same. It's just that you're talking about a different scale." (As Janssen McCormick, a 20-something FA from Massachusetts, puts it, "People send me links to articles about giant toothless women who get arrested for shoplifting turkeys under their boobs, and they're like, 'Hey, isn't that your type of gal?'" He sighs. "No, I don't find giant toothless ladies who steal turkeys under their boobs from Walmart hot.")

Misconception #4: Sex with a 110-pound woman is preferable to celibacy.

Not true. Lawrence says, "It's like, 'What, are you just going to go out and have sex with skinny women until you find a bigger one you like?' No, you're not. You're just going to stay home." (As Dan Weiss wrote on *Ask a Guy Who Likes Fat Chicks,* "With a sex life devoid of fat asses, I reckon I'd start coveting everyone I see leaving an Ashley Stewart or Walmart.")

Misconception #5: It's easy to pick up a fat chick.

Lawrence shakes his head. "A big girl at a bar tends to feel like there must be some sort of joke going on," he says. This is partly because the double-chinned woman in the hip-hiding shrug is so used to being ignored; partly because the specter of "hogging," the frat-boy prank practice of nailing a fat chick on a bro dare, casts a pall even on innocent flirting. "It's hard to be smooth when you're trying to convince someone that you're not playing a trick," Lawrence says. He's only met women out in a bar successfully once or twice. "Generally speaking, the odds are very much against you." (One 300-pound 30-something woman counters, "You have to be defensive because there are guys who are hogging, there are guys who are going to humiliate you. Also, it's internalized self-hatred, because you're like, 'If you like me, you must be a freak—why else would you like somebody who is fat?'")

Misconception #6: You've got to be kidding, right?

Nope. Lawrence, who sometimes fantasizes about a 550-pound wife, thinks the smallest he could go would be 180 pounds, though that veers into bisizualism. "Ideally, no. But you'd want to meet the girl's mother. If she's in her early twenties, and she's a hundred and eighty pounds, check out where it's going. You might be pleasantly surprised. You walk in and see her mom, and she's, like, really big, and you're, like, 'YES!' You're stoked. The genes don't lie." But she shouldn't be sloppy. "If the mom is in the muumuu, and she's just given up in life, you're like, 'Oh, shit.' You don't want that."

So where do Guys Who Like Fat Chicks meet them? Online, of course.

"The attention I'll get online is so much more frequent than what I experience in real life," says Jennifer Kronika, a 27-year-old 400-pound redhead living in Jacksonville, Florida. The men she's met and dated haven't been creeps. "These aren't weird guys. These aren't creepy 60-year-old guys with big bellies and fapping away behind their computers. These are totally normal guys."

"This is a community for people who feel differently," says Lawrence about FA-friendly forums like Dimensions or Curvage or various size-acceptance Facebook-group spin-offs. "These are communities that have become gathering places for those who have sort of shrugged off the yoke of self-loathing. You have to go to these safe areas where everyone has sort of been checked. 'Are you OK with yourself?' 'Are you OK with yourself?' OK, come on in."

Dear Askaguywholikesfatchicks:
What is the biggest/heaviest woman you have been with and did you have difficulty making love to her?
—Kelly Kyle
She was over 500 pounds and I don't recall any difficulty. I've had difficulty with women smaller than that, though. [June 24, 2010]

If you were at the Junior's Cheesecake in Times Square on the last Friday in March, say during the lunch rush between 1:30 and 3:00, and you happened to notice the 480ish-pound woman in a thin cardigan, halter top, and Internet-purchased pants presiding over a plate of corned beef and pastrami on rye with steak fries (which she didn't finish, but had wrapped), your first thought probably wasn't, Wow, I bet lots of men are into her. If you later witnessed the bespectacled girl coyly photograph her slice of strawberry-shortcake cheesecake to "make her friend Randy extremely jealous" or coquettishly rate the dessert as "not quite better than sex, but almost," you probably wouldn't have thought she'd have the opportunity to compare the two as soon as that night. If, after the check was paid, you saw her out front, sweetly struggling to climb into the SUV taxi, you probably didn't assume that she was heading back to the hotel to gussy herself up for a man who came from Europe to the United States specifically to be with her. "I just don't think people look at me at a restaurant and think, 'That girl has a really awesome dating life.'"

Yet that's the backstory on Charlotte, a 32-year-old from the South introduced as "five hundred pounds, but walking" who "gets hit on all the time." (She's employed by her Southern state government, and asked to be identified under a pseudonym.) In fact, the reason she is in New York for three nights, staying at the Candlewood Suites on West 39th, is a date. Several dates, actually—primarily with a 40-something immigration lawyer from Spain. But she also had a date last night, as it serendipitously turns out, with Lawrence, whom Charlotte has had a bit of a crush on for a while. She's looking for a longer-term commitment, though, and Lawrence honestly isn't, so "for me, he'd just be a really fun weekend," she says. Nothing transpired last night, though he did ask her to call him tomorrow if things didn't work out with the lawyer.

That would be Spanish Guy. Charlotte stutters, and certain words make the stammering worse, as does exhaustion, so "Spanish Guy" is easier to enunciate than her paramour's real name, even though she's bilingual. They've been flirting online regularly for five years. He has professed his love, but she's understandably wary since they'd never met in person until last night—after she went out with Lawrence. Their first encounter was awkward, she confesses. "He was just very nervous." The evening ended in her hotel room, but strictly under conversational pretenses; tired, she sent him off. "He starts walking toward the door, and then he turns, and gets bright red, and he's like, 'You don't like me as anything more than friends, do you?' And I just kind of looked at him. He was really serious. So I just yanked him over to me and kissed him." Then she sent him away. Tonight, they're going to MOMA ("He's really into art") and then a jazz club.

"There aren't many fat girls in Spain," reports Charlotte, who spent six months as an exchange student there in 2006. Back then, she weighed 425, and she claims that the department organizers at her Northeastern women's college tried to dissuade her from going abroad because she was "too big." She balked and went anyway, though she admits European daily life was far more taxing: The public bathrooms were "itty-bitty," the online clothes retailers she frequents didn't service Spain (Lane Bryant's sizes are too small for her), and walking was the primary method of transportation. "Anytime I would walk down the street, people would stare at me like I was a circus sideshow. Here, people kind of, like, glance out of the corner of their eye, but there people would stop and stare as I walked by."

One time in Spain, an old woman spotted Charlotte in public, stopped abruptly, and crossed herself. "Like I was Satan."

After walking four miles a day overseas, Charlotte lost 75 pounds, which she gained back upon return. And then some. Roller-coaster weight spikes and dips have steered her life since she was a small child. Her folks split when she was a "normal little healthy" two-year-old girl with dimples and Shirley Temple curls; she and her mother moved in with her grandparents. "Grandma always had body issues. She was probably about 225 or so and she always hated herself and was trying to lose weight and gaining it back," Charlotte says, apologizing for drawing the conversation into such solemn territory. "My mom worked really long hours, so Grandma was basically raising me. She put me on this diet and made me so small that my pediatrician said something to her. And then she would start feeding me what they ate, which was potatoes and junk food, until I got fat. Then she would put me on a diet again."

Charlotte is pretty sure that all the yo-yo dieting of her adolescence screwed up her metabolism permanently. Her first long-term boyfriend was a 21-year-old with "a little bit of a potbelly going on" whom she'd met online gaming. But after more than a year of having a 325-pound girlfriend, he caved to frat-boy peer pressure. "His friends couldn't stand the thought of one of their friends dating someone as fat as me," she confides matter-of-factly. "Finally, he said, 'You're going to have to lose weight, or we're going to have to break up.' And I loved him—I really loved him—so I really tried. I tried to lose weight, I tried dieting, I tried, and as with every diet I've ever been on, I ended up seventy-five pounds heavier than when I started. So that took me to four hundred twenty-five. And he broke up with me."

She's moved on, and in rather spectacular fashion. Scouring the Internet for plus-size clothes, she discovered BBW chat rooms when she was 18, and subsequently, a community of Fat Admirers who were rabidly attracted to her. Naturally, she explored this inverse reality, when it came time. "I had a rep—" she pauses to get the word out, "reputation for a little while. I did! I totally did! As a slut! I've been with seven people in my life. I do not feel that's excessive. I am extraordinarily picky, but I am not one of those women who plays games. If I want to sleep with a guy, I don't necessarily make him wait until the third date. We're adults!"

At the moment, she's not sure if she likes Spanish Guy "like that" or not. He's already called three times during lunch—his photo pops up when he rings, and the man pictured is a conventionally attractive man—but it was an hour earlier than she told him to call, so she shut off her phone. "What really pisses me off is the attitude that, like, that guy is dating below his league just because the girl he's dating is fat. And in fact, I may well be above his league," she says, laughing. "You can't know that, unless you know who I am."

Particularly infamous among the fat community is a *CSI* episode about a fat woman who has sex on top and kills her partner. "She was only two hundred fifty or three hundred pounds, or something like that," says Charlotte. "I have been five hundred pounds, and I would like to say that on top is my favorite position! I have not killed anybody yet." She smirks. "It's just interesting the way that society sees fat sexuality," she says. "It doesn't exist, or it kills you."

Dear Askaguywholikesfatchicks:
Is this because you think you can't do any better?
—BBB
Yes, but not in the way you're thinking.

"It's like one big boob." That's Dan Weiss's shorthand explanation for what it's like to be with fat women, what their bodies feel like naked, and the physical attributes he's found himself attracted to his entire life. If it sounds vulgar, well, that's the best way he can explain his fat attraction to other straight guys who express befuddlement and disgust. "It's the same property: men like fondling soft breasts, and I don't get why that doesn't apply to the whole body."

In many, many Western minds, it doesn't. Even the author of the 20th century's premier anthem to big ass doesn't like fat chicks. You know the one—"Baby Got Back," the 1992 Sir Mix-a-Lot hip-hop classic that blasts, proudly, defiantly: "I Like. Big. Butts! And I cannot lie!" Sure, the Seattle rapper addresses his desire to a woman with an "itty-bitty" waist planted atop a "real thick and juicy" backside, the provenance of Shakira wannabes and *King* magazine. But many Fat Admirers have adopted the anthem as their own. A rap-metal cover of the track appears, as part of a nether-region salute with a version of Ted Nugent's "Thunder Thighs," on last year's BBW-friendly compilation *WHOLE LOTTA LOVE: An All-Star Salute to Fat Chicks*.

According to Sir Mix-a-Lot himself (born Anthony Ray), fat-all-over is not what he meant. "I'm talking about the dumbbell shape. The Coke bottle," he clarifies over the phone from Atlanta. "I've seen girls that look like me and been like, 'Ohhhhh, I'm Baby's Got Back!' And I'm like, 'No, no, no, no.' It wasn't 'Baby Got Back and Center, and Middle, and Front.'" He does understand, though, why some of these FA fellows might get confused. "Obviously, more white people like the song than black. Black people kind of view 'Baby Got Back' as like, 'Oh, yeah, we already knew that.' It's not even an issue to them. They wouldn't even think to sing about it. Whereas white guys are kind of like,

'Yeah, finally!'"

Maybe so. Yet the cultural stigma of fat is spreading globally. Rapidly. Arizona State University researchers asked a group of subjects with an average body mass index (BMI) of 25 who reside in 10 countries including American Samoa, Puerto Rico, and Mexico—places where both fat and thin bodies have traditionally been seen as attractive—to assign true or false beliefs to cultural statements such as: "People should be proud of their big bodies" (false in every country surveyed but Tanzania) and "A big woman is a beautiful woman" (deemed false in every country). The standard medical response is that nearly all people with a BMI over 30 would be healthier at a lower weight. Alexandra Brewis, executive director of the School of Human Evolution and Social Change at Arizona State University, who oversaw the April 2011 study, says, "Fifteen years ago in American Samoa, fat bodies didn't have a negative salience, and that's shifted." She attributes this to the spread of American media and the moral implications of the War on Obesity. "A lot of people who didn't realize that they should be ashamed of their bodies are now probably learning to be."

"Fat is a risk factor," argues one 30-something New York–based physician who is African American and also identifies as a Fat Admirer. "It's also a proxy, but also an inaccurate proxy. Some people work out every day and are still fat; some people don't work out at all and are fat; some people don't work out at all and are skinny; some people work out a lot and are skinny. It's very individual. You can't be so declarative about it."

"One statistic I'd really like to know is how many people have banged a fat person," Dan Weiss says. "I've heard guys I know say, 'I wanna see what it's like to sleep with a five-hundred-pound woman.' There has to be some idea that it might feel good, or that it could be interesting to say that. You're not going to say, 'I'm going to sleep with a porcupine just to see what it's like.' It's not that I defend closet FAs, I'm just very interested in not dismissing them. Let's say half or more than half of the FA population is dormant and nothing is being done for them."

Dan likes to imagine a Guys Who Likes Fat Chicks census. "So many girls end up entering the community just because of one guy," he says. "Just discovering, 'Wow, I can be attractive!' and having that change your life. It just never occurred to them before, which is so weird." He pauses. "That's why I'm willing to put my life—if you want to call it that—on the line for this."

The Careless Language of Sexual Violence
Roxane Gay

There are crimes and then there are crimes and then there are atrocities. These are, I suppose, matters of scale. I read an article in the *New York Times* about an 11-year-old girl who was gang-raped by 18 men in Cleveland, Texas. The levels of horror to this story are many, from the victim's age to what is known about what happened to her, to the number of attackers, to the public response in that town, to how it is being reported. There is video of the attack, too, because this is the future. The unspeakable will be televised.

The *Times* article was titled, "Vicious Assault Shakes Texas Town," as if the victim in question was the town itself. James McKinley, Jr., the article's author, focused on how the men's lives would be changed forever, how the town was being ripped apart, how those poor boys might never be able to return to school. There was discussion of how the 11-year-old girl, the child,

dressed like a 20-year-old, implying that there is a realm of possibility where a woman can "ask for it" and that it's somehow
understandable that 18 men would rape a child. There were even
questions about the whereabouts of the mother, given, as we all
know, that a mother must be with her child at all times or whatever ill may befall the child is clearly the mother's fault. Strangely,
there were no questions about the whereabouts of the father while
this rape was taking place.

The overall tone of the article was what a shame it all was,
how so many lives were affected by this one terrible event. Little
of it addressed the girl, the child. It was an 11–year-old girl whose
body was ripped apart, not a town. It was an 11–year-old girl
whose life was ripped apart, not the lives of the men who raped
her. It is difficult for me to make sense of how anyone could lose
sight of that, and yet it isn't.

We live in a culture that is very permissive where rape is concerned. While there are certainly many people who understand
rape and the damage of rape, we also live in a time that neces-
sitates the phrase "rape culture." This phrase denotes a culture
where we are inundated, in different ways, by the idea that male
aggression and violence toward women is acceptable and often
inevitable. As Lynn Higgins and Brenda Silver ask in their book
Rape and Representation, "How is it that in spite (or perhaps because) of their erasure, rape and sexual violence have been so in-
grained and so rationalized through their representations as to appear 'natural' and inevitable, to women as well as men?" It is such
an important question, trying to understand how we have come
to this. We have also, perhaps, become immune to the horror of
rape because we see it so often and discuss it so often, many times
without acknowledging or considering the gravity of rape and its
effects. We jokingly say things like, "I just took a rape shower,"

or "My boss totally just raped me over my request for a raise." We have appropriated the language of rape for all manner of violations, great and small. It is not a stretch to imagine why James McKinley, Jr. is more concerned about the 18 men than one girl.

The casual way in which we deal with rape may begin and end with television and movies where we are inundated with images of sexual and domestic violence. Can you think of a dramatic television series that has not incorporated some kind of rape story line? There was a time when these story lines had a certain educational element to them, à la "A Very Special Episode." I remember, for example, the episode of *Beverly Hills 90210* where Kelly Taylor, surrounded tearfully by her closest friends, discussed being date-raped at a slumber party. For many young women, that episode created a space where they could have a conversation about rape as something that did not happen only with strangers. Later in the series, when the show was on its last legs, Kelly would be raped again, this time by a stranger. We watched the familiar trajectory of violation, trauma, disillusion, and finally vindication, seemingly forgetting that we had sort of seen this story before.

Half the movies aired on Lifetime or Lifetime Movie Network feature some kind of violence against women. The violence is graphic and gratuitous while still being strangely antiseptic: the actual act is more implied than shown. We consume these representations of violence eagerly. There is comfort, I suppose, in consuming violence in 90-minute segments, muted by commercials for household goods and communicated to us by former television stars with feathered bangs.

While rape as entertainment fodder may have included an element of the didactic at one time, such is no longer the case. Rape, these days, is good for ratings. *Private Practice*, a medical drama on ABC, recently aired a story arc where Dr. Charlotte King, iron-willed, independent, and sexually adventurous, was brutally raped. This happened, of course, just as February sweeps were beginning. The depiction of the assault was as graphic as you might expect from prime-time network television. For several episodes we saw the attack and its aftermath, how the once vibrant Charlotte became a shell of herself, how she became sexually frigid, how her body bore witness to the physical damage of rape. Another character on the show, Dr. Violet Turner, bravely confessed that she too had been raped. The show was widely applauded for its sensitive treatment of a difficult subject.

The soap opera *General Hospital* is currently airing a rape story line whose story arc peaked, yes, during sweeps. Like most soap operas, *General Hospital* incorporates a rape story line every five years or so when they need an uptick in viewers. Before the current rape, Emily Quartermaine was raped, and before Emily, Elizabeth Webber was raped, and long before Elizabeth Webber, Laura of Luke and Laura was raped by Luke but that rape was okay because Laura ended up marrying Luke so her rape doesn't really count. Every woman, *General Hospital* wants us to believe, loves her rapist. The current rape story line has a twist. This time the victim is a man, Michael Corinthos, Jr., son of Port Charles mob boss Sonny Corinthos, himself no stranger to violence against women. While it is commendable to see the show's producers trying to address the issue of male rape and prison rape, the subject matter is still handled carelessly, is still a source of titillation, and is still packaged neatly between commercials for cleaning products and baby diapers.

Of course, if we are going to talk about rape and how we are inundated by representations of rape and how, perhaps, we've become numb to rape, we have to discuss *Law & Order: SVU*, which deals, primarily, in sexual assault—all manner of sexual assault, against women, children, and once in a great while, men. Each week the violation is more elaborate, more lurid, more unspeakable. When the show first aired, Rosie O'Donnell objected quite vocally when one of the stars appeared on her show. O'Donnell said she didn't understand why such a show was needed. People dismissed her objections and the incident was quickly forgotten. The series is in its 12th season and shows no signs of ending anytime soon. When O'Donnell objected to *SVU*'s premise, when she dared to suggest that perhaps a show dealing so explicitly with sexual assault was unnecessary, was too much, people treated her as if she was the crazy one, the prude censor. I watch *SVU* religiously, have actually seen every single episode. I am not sure what that says about me.

It is rather ironic that only a couple weeks ago the *Times* ran an editorial about the War on Women. This topic is, obviously, one that matters to me. I recently wrote an essay about how, as a writer who is also a woman, I increasingly feel that to write is a political act—whether I intend it to be or not, because we live in a culture where McKinley's article is permissible and publishable. I am troubled by how we have allowed intellectual distance between violence and the representation of violence. We talk about rape but we don't talk about rape, not carefully.

We live in a strange and terrible time for women. There are days when I think it has always been a strange and terrible time to be a woman. It is nothing less than horrifying to realize we live in a culture where the "newspaper of record" can write an article that comes off as sympathetic to 18 rapists while encouraging victim blaming. Have we forgotten what an 11-year-old is? An 11-year-old is very, very young, and that amplifies the atrocity, at least for me. I also think that people perhaps do not understand the trauma of gang rape. While there's no benefit to creating a hierarchy of rape where one kind of rape is worse than another, because all rape is despicable, there is something particularly insidious about gang rape, about a pack of men feeding on each other's frenzy, individually and collectively acting on a belief that it is their right to violate a woman's body in such an unspeakable manner.

Gang rape is a difficult experience to survive physically and emotionally. There is the exposure to unwanted pregnancy and sexually transmitted diseases, vaginal and anal tearing, fistulas and vaginal scar tissue. The reproductive system is often irreparably damaged. Victims of gang rape, in particular, have a higher chance of miscarrying a pregnancy. Psychologically, there are any number of effects including PTSD, anxiety, fear, coping with the social stigma, coping with shame, and on and on. The actual rape ends but the aftermath can reach very far and be even more devastating than the rape itself. We rarely discuss these things, though. Instead, we are careless. We allow ourselves to believe that rape can be washed away as neatly as it is on TV and in the movies, where the trajectory of victimhood is neatly defined.

What I know about gang rape is that the experience is wholly consuming and a never-ending nightmare. There is little point in pretending otherwise. Perhaps James McKinley, Jr. is, like so many people today, anesthetized or somehow willfully distanced from such brutal realities. Perhaps despite this inundation of rape imagery, our immersion in a rape culture, not enough victims of gang rape speak out about the toll the experience exacts. Perhaps the right stories are not being told or we're not writing enough about the topic of rape. Perhaps we are writing too many stories about rape.

I approach this topic somewhat selfishly. I write about sexual violence a great deal in my fiction. I don't believe the why of this writerly obsession matters, but still, people often want to know what drives me to write these dark stories over and over. The why seems plainly obvious. I am trying to rewrite my own, difficult history as much as I try to write my way toward understanding how these things can happen, why they happen, why nothing changes. Perhaps it is simply that writing is cheaper than therapy or drugs. When I read articles such as McKinley's, I start to wonder about my responsibility as a writer. I'm just finishing my novel, the story of a brutal kidnapping in Haiti, part of which involves a gang rape. Having to write that kind of story requires going to a dark place. At times, I have made myself nauseous with what I'm writing and what I am capable of writing and imagining, my ability to go there.

As I write stories about sexual violence, I wonder if I am being gratuitous. I want to get it right. How do you get this sort of thing right? How do you write violence authentically without making it exploitative? There are times when I worry I am contributing to the kind of cultural numbness that would allow an article like the one in the *Times* to be written and published, that allows rape to be such rich fodder for popular culture and entertainment. No matter how hard we try, we cannot separate violence in fiction from violence in the world. As Laura Tanner notes in her book *Intimate Violence*, "The act of reading a representation of violence is defined by the reader's suspension between the semiotic and the real, between a representation and the material dynamics of violence which it evokes, reflects, or transforms." She continues, "The distance and detachment of a reader who must leave his or her body behind in order to enter imaginatively into the scene of violence make it possible for representations of violence to obscure the material dynamics of bodily violation, erasing not only the victim's body but his or her pain." The way we currently represent rape, in books, in newspapers, on television, on the silver screen, often allows us to ignore the material realities of rape, the impact of rape, the meaning of rape.

While I have these concerns, I also feel committed to telling the truth, to saying these violences happen even if bearing such witness contributes to a spectacle of sexual violence. When we're talking about race or religion or politics, it is often said we need to speak carefully. With these difficult topics we need to be vigilant not only in what we say but how we express ourselves. That same care, I would suggest, has to be extended to how we write about violence, and sexual violence in particular.

The *Times* article uses the phrase "sexual assault," and includes the phrase "the girl had been forced to have sex with several men." The word *rape* is only used twice and not within the context of the victim's experience. This is not the careful use of language. In this instance, and far more often than makes sense, language is used to buffer our sensibilities from the brutality of rape, from the extraordinary nature of such a crime.

Feminist scholars have long called for a rereading of rape. Higgins and Silver note that "the act of rereading rape involves more than listening to silences; it requires restoring rape to the literal, to the body: restoring, that is, the violence—the physical, sexual violation." I would suggest we need to find new ways, whether in fiction or creative nonfiction or journalism, not only to reread rape but to rewrite rape as well—ways of rewriting that restore the actual violence to these crimes, that make it impossible for men to be excused for committing these atrocities, that make it impossible for articles like McKinley's to be written, to be published, to be considered acceptable.

An 11-year-old girl was raped by 18 men. The suspects ranged in age from middle-schoolers to a 27-year-old. There are pictures and videos. Her life will never be the same. The *New York Times*, however, would like you to worry about those boys, who will have to live with this for the rest of their lives. This is not simply the careless language of violence. It is the criminal language of violence.

Men Who "Buy Sex" Commit More Crimes: Newsweek, Trafficking, and the Lie of Fabricated Sex Studies

Thomas Roche

An old-school radical antiporn, antiprostitution activist known for criminal antics is in the news again, portraying a heavily biased anti–sex work survey[1] as science, when in fact it's the same message Melissa Farley has been screaming her entire career. Sadly, press outlets like *Newsweek*,[2] Reuters,[3] Jezebel,[4] and the *Sydney Morning Herald*[5] are taking the bait, ignoring the fact that their information comes from a dubious report by a biased organization putting out a press release on PR Newswire[6]—a for-pay distribution service that features relatively little other than self-promoting garbage.

News outlets are treating the information as if it's from a scientist, or a social sciences organization, or an objective source, or as if it's based on anything like a real study. It's not any of those things.

The "report" is really a series of prejudicial interpretations of a prejudiced in-person survey made by an openly biased researcher who has spent her entire career pushing this same point: summarizing "research" funded by an organization that has no earthly purpose other than to eliminate prostitution by any means possible.

Melissa Farley, the first author on the "report," which was presented on July 15, 2011, at a meeting of Psychologists for Social Responsibility, is probably most famous for claiming that call girls are no less damaged than street prostitutes by their experiences of sex work. Farley was arrested 13 times in the 80s for defacing bookstore copies of *Penthouse*; her account of that crusade appeared in an article titled "Fighting Femicide in the United States: The Rampage Against *Penthouse*."

Farley's latest bit of activism is a "report" of a survey—incorrectly called a "study"—that recruited 202 men to answer questions in person. About half of the men "buy sex" and the rest do not. In Farley's parlance, "buying sex" means frequenting prostitutes. The use of the term *buying* is insulting. It's a transparent attempt by Farley to conflate human trafficking with prostitution, and she's been doing it her whole career.

But that equation is garbage; it's meant to differentiate between nonsex services and sex, as a way of taking the agency out of women's hands and placing it squarely in the hands of—whom? Farley? No, damn it—men. Not to get too 70s about it, but wasn't that why I became a sensitive New Age guy to begin with? So the women I knew could stop having their power taken away?

For what I hope will be the last time but I know will not, let's get it straight: If you can "buy" sex from a sex worker, then you can "buy" therapy from a clinical psychologist and "buy" accounting from an accountant.

Sex is not a thing, it is a behavior—or, rather, a series of behaviors, with an endless gray area between where one behavior ends and another begins. If you agree with me on only one point in this discussion, let it be that sex is not a thing.

Women are not notches that guys carve in their bedposts (or on the dashboards of their Chevelles). One does not "acquire" sex from a woman, and the suggestion that one does is equivalent to saying that a woman's virtue is a finite quantity that can be taken away.

Farley knows this, but she also knows that you get better sound bites by claiming, explicitly, that slavery and prostitution are not just related, they are literally the same. Seriously. She claims that there is no difference, in the same way she has claimed that there is no difference between the experience of the streetwalker and the experience of the call girl or brothel worker. This concept is frankly insulting to anyone who's ever been friends with a woman who walked the street.

But Farley feels a need to equate the trafficked juvenile in Thailand with the $500-an-hour call girl. In so doing, she's engaging in the inexplicable cognitive disconnect that alienates so many otherwise right-thinking women in my generation from Feminism with a capital F; she's convinced herself that by speaking of concrete social issues as if they were cultural abstractions, she can achieve an impossible social agenda, as Andrea Dworkin hoped to do by saying that "penetrative intercourse is, by its nature, violent."[7]

Farley's conclusions in the new "survey" should therefore surprise no one. According to her highly biased claims, men who "buy sex" have a greater predisposition to rape, less respect for women, and are more likely to have committed crimes than men who do not buy sex.

A survey, incidentally, is not the same as a study. A study is a formalized procedure for obtaining concrete and measurable data, with steps taken to ensure that compared data sets are equivalent.

In my opinion, social sciences surveys are worth nothing at all. They're like marketing focus groups. They show a fantastic tendency to display interviewer bias.

Good surveys are transparent about what questions are asked and how they are asked. They don't come with foregone conclusions established by the bias of the lead author. They are not funded by organizations with a stated goal of eliminating the behavior they are asking questions about. And even good surveys are still just surveys. In the case of qualitative data—for instance, how well or sick chemotherapy patients are feeling—steps are taken to eliminate interviewer bias. There's no indication that such steps have been taken in Farley's survey; in fact, given Farley's track record, it seems clear that they have not.

But still, plenty of news agencies find some "interesting results" here—as if there were any results at all, other than Melissa Farley repeating the same histrionic, man-hating screed that she's been howling since the 80s.

Nah, don't worry about the fact that the results come from one of the most virulent anti–sex work, antiporn activists, one who displays a serious lack of transparency in her survey procedures. Why should you? *Newsweek* sure didn't. *Newsweek*'s piece was originally titled "The Growing Demand for Prostitution," but apparently somebody objected so they changed the title to "The John Next Door." Smart move, since their smokescreen of terror is based on a report that does not address whether there is in fact a rising incidence of prostitution.

The following quote is from the *Newsweek* article "The John Next Door":

> The men who buy sex are your neighbors and colleagues. A new study reveals how the burgeoning de-

mand for porn and prostitutes is warping personal relationships and endangering women and girls.

Men of all ages, races, religions, and backgrounds do it. Rich men do it, and poor men do it, in forms so varied and ubiquitous that they can be summoned at a moment's notice.

And yet surprisingly little is known about the age-old practice of buying sex, long assumed to be inevitable. No one even knows what proportion of the male population does it; estimates range from 16 percent to 80 percent. "Ninety-nine percent of the research in this field has been done on prostitutes, and 1 percent has been done on johns," says Melissa Farley, director of Prostitution Research and Education, a nonprofit organization that is a project of San Francisco Women's Centers.[8]

Does anyone else spot the fallacy here? "Men of all ages, races, religions and backgrounds do it," "... in forms so varied and ubiquitous that they can be summoned in a moment's notice," "And yet surprisingly little is known about the age-old practice of buying sex." If it's so common, how is it that "surprisingly little is known about it?" Or is it just that those who know about it aren't important—because they're not people? But now Melissa Farley has talked to those inhuman monsters—and she knows what horrible misogynist thoughts these inhuman drooling beasts are thinking when they buy sex.

Newsweek's credulity also underlines Farley's dynamic in choosing two quotes from survey participants as the subtitle of the report:

One man in the study explained why he likes to buy prostitutes: "You can have a good time with the servitude," he said. A contrasting view was expressed by another man as the reason he doesn't buy sex: "You're supporting a system of degradation," he said.

If this dualism seems familiar to you, it's the same double standard women have been subjected to for the whole of human history. Are you the Madonna or the whore? Do you "buy sex," or do you respect women?

If the assertion that most or nearly all men do this but "nothing is known about it" also sounds familiar, it's the Victorian split that feminism rightly objected to in social sciences, particularly in Freud and his followers. It's just been turned around to face *men*. In one of his most egregiously sexist statements, Freud said: "The great question that has never been answered, and which I have not yet been able to answer, despite my thirty years of research into the feminine soul, is 'What does a woman want?'"

Freud famously treated women as "other." This was a way of shaming their desires and dehumanizing them. It was necessary for someone—Freud, or another male social scientist—to "understand these strange creatures" before that understanding could enter the body of human knowledge. That's because, to Freud—as to many if not most male social scientists before feminism—women were not people.

Men who buy sex are not people to Farley—or to *Newsweek*, apparently. Farley sold them a prize plucked from the jaws of woman-hating Victorian sexuality, having transposed the Madonna/whore and watcher/watched dichotomies onto the male experience. By turning her outrage on men, Farley is silencing women just as upper-middle-class white feminists, and particularly feminist social scientists, have long been accused of doing. This is not science; it's a vendetta against male sexuality, cherry-picking the very worst examples as horror stories to create a pathology that includes all men—and any women who don't think and behave exactly the way Farley wants them to.

Reuters does an even more half-assed job of "reporting" on Farley's "research" in an article that's been reprinted in many news outlets and cut and pasted frequently, probably because it's got such a catchy and easy-to-understand headline: "Men Who Buy Sex Commit More Crimes, Report Says."

> Men who pay for sex are more likely than men who do not pay for sex to commit a variety of offenses including violent crimes against women, according to research conducted in the Boston area.
>
> Men who paid for sex were more likely to report having committed felonies and misdemeanors, including crimes related to violence against women and those related to substance abuse, assault and weapons, the study found.
>
> The study was designed, among other things, to test attitudes of men who buy sex. It found that as a group, they share certain attitudes and behavioral tendencies different from their nonbuying peers.
>
> Almost three in four of the sex buyers reported they learned about sex from pornography, whereas only 54 percent of the nonbuyers did so.
>
> The two groups also held significantly different attitudes regarding whether prostitution was consenting sex or exploitation. Men who bought sex were significantly less empathetic toward women working as

prostitutes.

Two thirds of both groups concluded most women prostitutes had been lured, tricked or trafficked into the work.

But sex buyers "seemed to justify their involvement in the sex industry by stating their belief … that women in prostitution were intrinsically different from nonprostituting women," the study's authors said.[9]

It hurts my brain to think that someone at Reuters could have written this with a straight face: "The study was designed, among other things, to test attitudes of men who buy sex. It found that as a group, they share certain attitudes and behavioral tendencies different from their nonbuying peers."

No, no, no. The study was most explicitly *not* designed to "test attitudes of men who buy sex." It was designed to prove that they have objectionable attitudes toward women. Period. Farley has been trying to do this in every way she can imagine for her entire career. Her nonprofit Prostitution Research and Education[10] does not do research or promulgate education; it seeks to eliminate all sex work through any means necessary. And this survey, conducted in Boston, was funded by the Hunt Alternatives Fund, a group that started in the 80s with the goal of nuclear disarmament through Hunt's pet project, Demand Abolition. According to the landing page at Hunt, "Demand Abolition supports the movement to end modern-day slavery by combating the demand for illegal commercial sex in the US. By conducting and disseminating research, educating policymakers, providing technical assistance to criminal justice professionals, and convening key stakeholders, Demand Abolition is catalyzing systemic social change that reflects the dignity of all people."[11]

The page redirects you to the new Demand Abolition page, which states: "Until we eliminate demand, the sexual enslavement of our society's most vulnerable children, women, and even men will continue unabated."[12]

At the landing page for its FAQs, Demand Abolition states: "In simple question and answer format, the Coalition Against Trafficking in Women has issued a clarion call to end prostitution and sex trafficking by criminalizing and penalizing buyers of sex."[13]

Wait—Demand Abolition wants to "demand abolition"? It wants to "criminalize" the buying of sex? Are they joking? Buying sex is already illegal in most places—and it also exists almost everywhere. But this group is actually claiming that it must be "criminalized"? How far out of the world we live in do you have to be where you can believe that prostitution hasn't been criminalized?

The answer? You just have to be a radical antisex feminist, apparently. In which case male-dominated society looks like just one big blur. Equating a law enforcement structure that can't manage to stamp out street prostitution with men who frequent call girls and politicians who don't pass stronger laws is only possible if men aren't people.

What's more, the places where sex work is most illegal (Saudi Arabia and other Sharia-governed states) are without exception the places where it's most dysfunctional (e.g., trafficked women). The nations with the harshest antiprostitution laws are the one with the greatest social strictures against consensual sexual encounters between men and women. Those countries are also— and this isn't an accident—the nations where there's the greatest difference between rich and poor, and the places where women have the lowest status. Oppressive laws disproportionately affect the poor, women, and racial, ethnic, and religious minorities, no matter what those laws are passed to accomplish.

But it gets worse. The "hooker-free Utopia" Farley wants to see in the United States is even more extreme than she'd let you know. Arab countries like Saudi Arabia and Egypt have a documented constancy of homosexual rape in both social and penal circumstances, as well as antigay murder of anyone who isn't "discreet" about same-sex contacts.

My favorite example of this is related in Robert Lacey's *Inside the Kingdom*:[14] a Saudi man is sent to prison for marrying his Filipino houseboy—this in a country where same-sex contact is common because the sexes are so thoroughly segregated. In a different case related in the same book, a Shi'ite woman living in a Shi'ite majority community in the Gulf was abducted and gang-raped by Sunni youths, then sent to prison because she had "asked for it" by meeting a man at the mall to demand the return of a (nonnude, fully clothed) photograph of her that a friend had given him. She wanted it back for fear that she would be considered "loose" if the photo got out.

In Cairo, according to British journalist John R. Bradley's excellent book *Inside Egypt,*[15] male–male rape by police officers, often of male children who have at best committed minor offenses, has resulted in a terrorized young male populace. I have no idea if it's changed since the revolution, but I doubt it. These are the kinds of societies that vigorously prosecute prostitution.

But let's not blame the Muslims; in Thailand, India, Brazil, the Philippines, and many other nations, rampant sex trafficking occurs, including sex tourism from Western countries—despite prostitution being entirely illegal (Thailand, the Philippines, Russia, Ukraine, etc.) or brothels and pimping being illegal (Brazil, India, Kazakhstan, etc). The governments of India and

Thailand—and more recently Brazil[16]—are constantly trumpeting new legal measures to prevent sex trafficking, in order to court US investment—despite the fact that trafficking is rampant. Trafficking continues because of corruption and poverty, not because there are no laws against it.

The worst-case scenario for sex trafficking and child exploitation is a corrupt society where laws are enforced not based on criminal activity, but on the divide between rich and poor—and manipulation of the media plays a strong role. Yet for trafficking and child exploitation, nothing seems to change in the long run, except that it gets worse. The countries with the greatest poverty, corruption, and restrictions on personal behavior are the places where trafficking runs rampant, because the law is enforced with not just a double standard, but a predictably privilege-based standard. It's based on the social position of the client and the amount of money that changes hands—not from john to sex worker, but from john to authorities, from pimp to authorities, from sex worker to authorities. The idea that in poor and corrupt countries such a situation will be solved if we "abolish" prostitution by putting the names of johns in the paper (as Farley claims) is utterly laughable. Corrupt nations mostly already have strong antiprostitution laws. It's poverty and corruption that need to be "abolished."

But that's not Demand Abolition's view. Want to know where they locate the worst-case scenario for prostitution laws? Not Burma, not India, not Sudan—but Australia. " ... a wave of sex trafficking and other ills always follows the legalization of prostitution. For instance, parts of Australia have experimented with decriminalization and witnessed skyrocketing illegal prostitution because the buyers still want to purchase children, 'exotic' women from abroad, and sex acts that may be off-limits in the legal venues."[17]

Farley and her cronies actually believe the circumstances for prostitutes are the very worst in *Australia*? Because Australia, they claim, "witnessed skyrocketing illegal prostitution," that means we should "abolish" prostitution everywhere? Like, say, all the places where it's already illegal? Because that hasn't resulted in skyrocketing prostitution, unless you believe the *Newsweek* article about Farley's study. (In case you forgot, it was headlined "The Growing Demand for Prostitution" until *Newsweek* chickened out and changed it, because neither they nor Farley could convincingly make a data-based case that there *is* a growing demand for prostitution. Better to call it "The John Next Door," creating the impression that sex work patrons live right next to you, lurking, waiting for you to look the other way so you won't see them drive off to visit a hooker.)

But does that mean *Newsweek* is talking only about countries where it's legal (plus those eight counties in Nevada)? I mean, *Newsweek* is an American magazine, and prostitution is mostly illegal here. Because if there's a "growing demand for prostitution" in places where prostitution is illegal—gasp, could that mean...?

Or do *Newsweek* and Demand Abolition not have the faintest idea whether there's a growing demand for prostitution, because they wouldn't know actual data if it bit 'em on the ass and then charged 'em $5? Does Demand Abolition not know what they believe—other than that they object to the very fact of prostitution, and will make up social trends, statistics, and facts at will?

Incidentally, if Australia is Demand Abolition's worst-case scenario, what's their best case? Sweden. "The primer also takes note of promising results coming out of Sweden, where a 1999 law decriminalized the sale of sex but rigorously enforced a ban on purchasing it. Since passage, the number of women forced into street prostitution has fallen by 50 percent."[18]

So it's legal to sell, but illegal to buy? How does that work, exactly, in terms of teaching your kids what's legal to do and not to do? Or is it already assumed that nobody of value would ever let their son or daughter buy or sell sex?

As I suggested above, the exceptions are poor women and rich men. Rich men enlisting the services of poor women usually gets a blind eye, no matter what country and what aeon they're in. That equation is sacrosanct and will remain so until we eliminate economics entirely. That's why any enforcement activity against sex work always disproportionately impacts poor sex workers, and any enforcement activity against clients always disproportionately affects those who frequent poorer sex workers—especially, but not exclusively, lower-middle-class, working-class, and poor men who can't afford to pay $200 or $300 for sex.

Rich men are never going to lose their options for hiring sex workers. In the Victorian era, just as in Saudi Arabia, just as in Washington, DC, all you have to do is this: Be male, have plenty of money, and exercise a culturally appropriate degree of discretion, and you can always find a woman who'll fuck you. That is not going to change, no matter what country you're in, what era you're in or what law enforcement actions are taken. But what *can* change is how many poor sex workers face arrest, rape, and prison time because of hysterical prohibitionist panic based on bad science.

Farley's campaign is aimed at wealthy Western nations, and therein lies the rub. She seems willing to haul the trafficked Cambodian children out of their rail container and parade them around in the White People's Tragedy Tourism Dance whenever it helps her argue for stronger antiprostitution laws in Nevada. Farley is happy to equate third-world human trafficking with heroin-addicted women in Los Angeles with high-class hookers and strippers who occasionally give a blow job in the back room for $300. But she has yet to establish that any parallel can be drawn between these scenarios using any weapon other than the anti-male, antisex, and ultimately antifemale brand of helpless-woman feminism that was rejected by the vast majority of American women 20 years ago. In doing so, Farley is snug in bed with the most right-wing, reactionary elements in America who, if they could have their way, would have her and her fellow feminists in the kitchen baking casseroles.

Let us reject Farley's bankrupt and transparently sexist claim that sex is a thing women own and that men take away—by purchasing it or by stealing it or by pressuring them into giving it up or by marrying them.

Sex is not a thing.

It's not women's job to "keep" sex so that people like Melissa Farley will approve of them. And it's not the habit of men with hard dicks to follow anybody's idea of morality except their own. For the record, plenty of us *do* manage to make it through life without violating our own codes of morality, which are apparently far more complex than Farley's since they allow for female personal agency. This is what makes so reprehensible Farley's attempt to enforce a single, extraordinarily restrictive moral behavior for men—despite the clear evidence that poverty is what creates despair, that drugs, abuse, and lack of opportunity go where poverty goes, and that these elements together create the most dysfunctional sex work environments. Those dysfunctions will not be eliminated by decriminalization of prostitution—certainly not street prostitution—but they sure as fuck aren't going to be eliminated by Farley's unsupportable ivory-tower sex-hating hysteria.

Why should I care? A few hysterical articles in the press, some dumb ideas in action, the slow erosion and discrediting of the social sciences—nothing we haven't seen before, right? But Farley's unsupported claims and the ease with which the press picked them up are evidence of the building feedback loop of antisex hysteria. More important, it's just this kind of histrionic, crazy doublethink that alienated women of my generation from the idea of Feminism, capital F, or feminism, small f, as something they could see in themselves. I'm tired of seeing women my age afraid to call themselves feminists.

Every time I hear a woman my age or younger say, "I'm not a feminist, but…" I thank Melissa Farley.

Endnotes

1 www.demandabolition.org/how-we-work/groundbreaking-research/boston-sex-buyers-report/
2 www.thedailybeast.com/newsweek/2011/07/17/the-growing-demand-for-prostitution.html
3 www.reuters.com/article/2011/07/20/us-usa-prostitution-idUS-TRE76J39N20110720
4 http://jezebel.com/5822905/men-who-pay-for-sex-also-in-debt-to-society
5 www.smh.com.au/lifestyle/lifematters/blogs/citykat/whats-the-real-price-of-selling-sex-20110719-1hmws.html
6 www.prnewswire.com/news-releases/demand-abolition-prostitution-is-not-a-victimless-crime-125801573.html
7 www.snopes.com/quotes/mackinnon.asp
8 www.thedailybeast.com/newsweek/2011/07/17/the-growing-demand-for-prostitution.html
9 www.reuters.com/article/2011/07/20/us-usa-prostitution-idUS-TRE76J39N20110720
10 www.prostitutionresearch.com/c-prostitution-men-who-buy-sex.html
11 www.huntalternatives.org/pages/7902_demand_abolition.cfm
12 www.demandabolition.org/
13 www.demandabolition.org/why-demand/primer-on-demand/
14 www.goodreads.com/book/show/6484927-inside-the-kingdom
15 www.goodreads.com/book/show/2994443-inside-egypt
16 www.gainesvilletimes.com/archives/52951/
17 www.demandabolition.org/why-demand/primer-on-demand/
18 www.demandabolition.org/why-demand/primer-on-demand/

Taking Liberties
Tracy Quan

This feature appeared in *Marie Claire Malaysia*, June 2011. Reprinted with permission from Marie Claire Malaysia: http://www.marieclaire.com.my/

As a first-time hooker working in the London hotel bars, I quickly discovered that the super-rich trophy client can be a claustrophobic companion. My fantasies were about freedom, not wealth. While I enjoyed the high-end scene, I often preferred working the middle of the market.

Belinda, one of the girls I looked up to, had a rich Saudi client who used his generosity to monopolize her. While it sounds romantic to hit the jackpot in this way, there was way too much drama. In contrast, I had Stanley, an easygoing salesman from Leicester who never questioned a working girl's freedom. Stanley couldn't afford to buy me a flat, but Belinda's situation made me wonder: why should a wealthy client behave in ways we'd consider psychotic in a middle-class man?

Stanley was a lot like the warm businesslike customers I met when I moved to New York. The escort service I worked for wasn't exactly high class, but a steady diet of high-class dudes can get boring. The parade of men from every class, religion, and ethnic group turned my job into an informal sociology course. I met self-made billionaires, celebs, art dealers, movers and shakers—but I also met the indentured restaurant worker, the dentist, the furniture salesman, an air-conditioner repairman. It was tremendously liberating to know I could relate to such a wide range of men, that I didn't have to spend all night—like Belinda—with a controlling millionaire.

One of the silliest misconceptions about my former profession is the assumption that every call girl prefers to be a high-end courtesan. The less well-to-do clients sensed that I had other options, so they felt lucky to have a brief encounter. An appointment could last 15 minutes or five hours, depending on the type of client I saw.

Among my first New York customers was a bachelor in working-class Washington Heights, one of many African American soldiers who had gone to Europe when the United States was still segregated. My transatlantic accent reminded him of his army years. He hadn't been back to England after the war, but he had good memories. Impeccably polite and courtly, he came very quickly. I was new to the business, while he had been seeing prostitutes for years. He was comfortable with the transaction—neither cold nor sentimental—and made me feel a bit like a goddess for 20 minutes.

Later that night I was sent to the Waldorf-Astoria Hotel, where my client was a white, well-off, married Midwesterner. My last client that night was 30-something and Jewish, a single guy with frizzy hair in a renovated Upper East Side tenement down the street from an expensive-looking high-rise. He smoked pot and used a lot of black American jargon to flirt with me. What a funny charmed place New York was turning out to be.

When I graduated from the escort agency to work with a group of successful call girls, those earlier customers could no longer afford my new rate. I was comfortable with my roster of swanky clients, but I often felt that my encounters with less wealthy guys were more interesting.

Ten years later I compared notes with Belinda, who never left the circle of the very rich. Though she had been successful from the start, she hated her job and felt stuck. Traveling between the high end and the middle market seemed like a compromise to her, but not to me. If a wealthy customer wanted to spend eight hours doing illegal drugs in his five-star hotel room, I could opt out. I could see, instead, a nice dentist or accountant with only an hour to spare and no portable drug habit. On a good day I might have sex with five ordinary customers instead of one megadate. My body got more of a workout, but when I did a midnight call with a demanding zillionaire, I felt free to leave early.

You might wonder how a girl with a distinctive look migrates between different price cliques. In a conventional job, a person who keeps changing her name would be viewed as a nut, but it's more than okay in sex work to alter your identity—as long as you maintain a spotless rep. (If you adopt a new name simply to cheat people, word gets around.) Madams routinely accepted the fact that I used three or four names, and I felt privileged reinventing myself on a regular basis.

If you're willing to entertain a higher volume of men, if you aren't horrified by a client who works a blue-collar job, you have more options than the girl with a fetish about catching a big fish. A girl who sees 10 working-class men each day is often stereotyped as a victim. Actually, she may feel more independent this way and dislike making small talk with the rich and famous. I've known girls who felt trapped and unhappy operating at the top of the market, while some of the most cheerful sex workers I've met have been streetwalkers or brothel workers. The wealthiest men may be spoiled, used to getting their way.

In my job, I had an opportunity to mingle with girls from everywhere. My co-workers were unschooled drug users who ran away on the bus to New York, nerdy medical students, boarding-school babes who sold real estate by day and sex by night, semi-employed musicians, mysterious vagabonds. I met girls who had pimps and girls who lived entirely alone. Some were sex addicts, others nearly frigid. Most kept the job a secret from family members—but I also knew two sisters who saw clients together. Too many people, even in a city as colorful as New York, consort with a narrow predictable group. Not me.

Women enter the sex trade for many reasons. It's a myth that we're all addicted to Louis Roederer Cristal, pricey lingerie, and Prada. Sometimes we work just enough to pay our bills, so we can have time for our hobbies. Material wealth, I found, was quite alluring to girls who had grown up poor.

Gigi, who came from a rough neighborhood, was brilliant at saving money and sometimes worked around the clock, sleeping in a loft bed high above the mattress and box spring that was reserved for sex with clients. Karen, who spent nights in a home-less shelter when her parents were divorcing, was another savvy investor. She used prostitution as a ladder to middle-class security. I sometimes envy their solid financial goals.

For me, having grown up middle class, with neither deprivation nor luxury, prostitution was an elusive, occasionally confusing pursuit of something harder to define. Personal autonomy, the liberty to make my own mistakes and be answerable to myself—in a word, freedom.

And yet I'm different from the college girl escorts and middleclass sex workers you so often hear about. As a teenager under the legal working age, I yearned for the freedoms enjoyed by legal adults. I had to fight (albeit covertly) for the right to work at all. I landed my first office gig during my 13th summer by lying about my age, only to be fired after two weeks when they found out. For a kid so obsessed with the right to work, running away at 14, dropping out of high school, and turning tricks was logical. When a boyfriend tried to persuade me that I should quit, I felt the walls closing in on me.

I was thumbing my nose at conventional feminism, which creates a straitjacket for young women, urging us to be good girls who finish school, go to university, and pursue a career where you keep respectable hours. I am, by nature, a night owl, and feminism seemed to favor the early riser.

As a junior hooker, I was delighted to find you could start your workday around three or four in the afternoon. Exploring central London at night, I was seduced by the opportunity to live with my natural body clock. But freedom at 14 is a bright, shiny object. You don't realize that it comes with a price.

When I began working in my own flat, the easiest customers turned out to be morning appointments. These 10:00 a.m. guys were eager to get back to work, so their sexual demands were simple. They were happy to let me initiate sex without trying to explore my body, and quite a few were satisfied with some quick oral sex or a hand job. A more demanding type will wait until he has a block of time to indulge himself.

The later you rise, the more complicated and tactile the customers become. Clients who party with escorts in the evening want to chat for hours, play with your emotional boundaries (not to mention your clitoris), and get to know you. I wasn't always in the mood for this.

If you prefer to work in a well-managed brothel with high turnover and less mental involvement, you may have to get up rather early! The freedom to set your own hours means answering your own phone, managing a business. You end up working harder because you're always strategizing. You become, in essence, your own madam, but the hard work was worth it to me.

I was glad to have multiple sex partners, sometimes as many as eight in one day.

Having sex with men you're not attracted to is actually quite interesting—even though it sounds horrible to the average modern woman. The liberated Western lifestyle encourages us to objectify men, but when you lust after a man—imitating the male gaze by turning it around on him—you lose touch with the classical narcissism that brings pleasure to a prostitute. Sex with a man you're not into forces you to become a star in the bedroom, where you project shameless self-love. Much as I enjoyed this, I've never been able to carry my vampy industrial personality into my love life: it's very specific to commercial sex.

I also enjoyed getting to know men and women outside my age group. In so many jobs and corporations, people are clumped together in age ghettos where 20-somethings have only superficial contact with people in their fifties or sixties. At 19, I routinely had female mentors of 45, 50, or 60 who spoke candidly about sex, love, life, and the law.

Getting naked with a man old enough to be my grandfather made me feel like his social equal. My customers also experienced some temporary freedom—stepping outside their nine-to-five selves to be with a confident young girl who wasn't afraid to kid around or act familiar.

A 40ish madam told me why she wasn't turned on by women: "They don't have that thing between their legs. But don't shelter yourself—everyone should try it." I had, since age 13, defined myself as bisexual, but didn't get a chance to find out until I became a New York call girl. Three-way sex (two girls, one man) was rampant. All the girls encouraged it, to give a customer variety without losing his business. A madam could double her income and keep two girls busy. Some girls wanted to fake it; some were into the real thing. When two girls didn't see eye to eye, there was paranoia, disgust—or just wry laughter.

My friend Suzy had a way to deal with this. "I'm not into girls, but I'm happy to do it for real if your customer wants it." This was my policy, too. I had a few friends I enjoyed working with, because we tend to be good at things we like doing—especially where oral sex is concerned. Making another girl come while someone else is paying: does it mean you're gay if you keep inviting her back to see the same client? I enjoyed sex with a woman—sometimes when servicing a married couple—but the idea of going steady with a girl made me uncomfortable. There was no pressure to declare myself gay or straight, and when I left the industry, I had no interest in girl-sex at all. Coincidence? Or proof that I'm gay for pay? I've never been sure.

And speaking of orgasms, they are a misunderstood perk of the job. Paid sex is one way to have an orgasm without strings attached, but nobody enters the business for the sex alone. I had my first multiple orgasms with one of my clients. Still in my teens, I learned about sex on the job and found that my body had its own agenda. Don't assume that multiples are typical, though. You aren't normally that relaxed at work, but having sex every day brings you to a point where your body can't stand it anymore—unless you come. Sometimes it's a relief to do this with a man who doesn't know your real name, age, or address.

And when you enjoy a high level of sexual freedom, you can discover that the most delicious connection to have with a man is traditional vanilla.

Why Lying about Monogamy Matters
Susie Bright

Op-ed columnist Ross Douthat has written an argument for the *New York Times* titled "Why Monogamy Matters." He says that women with minimal or virginal sexual experience are the happiest women in the land. Wheeeee! Upon the story's publication, pink-cheeked schoolgirls in braids floated across the national horizon, clutching bouquets of daisies, giggling over something they couldn't quite recall. Happy. Happy! That's what little girls are made of. Ross knows.

According to Douthat, back in the old days (before women's lib), Americans had far less premarital sex, and they married when they were really old, after they'd considered everything, like their moral values. So happy, too, really happy. It's in all the historical record; I'm sure he checked! Ross reminds us that no matter what you hear today, abstinence programs really work. Do you know how happy that makes him? Tee-hee! Ross always makes me laugh, and that makes me—happy!

There are Four Big Kinds of Sex: casual, promiscuous, premature, and ill-considered. They all lead to—depression. Did you know that? It's truthy. Ross looked it all up in a book by a Christian sociologist in Texas who has studied things like "pornography," and its magical ability to wed grown men to masturbation for the rest of their lives, to the exclusion of any real, live yummy sex partners. Fascinating stuff.

Douthat teaches us that sexual restraint leads to "emotional well-being." Restraint is another word for: happiness! Not knowing too much is the biggest happiness of all. Little girls crave security, that's what you have to understand. Bunnies. Baa-Baa. Binkies! Mommmmy!

Little boys—I'm not sure what Ross says they care about—except that hot porno the other guy mentioned. I'm sure he'll write about them next time.

Little gay or trans people—HEY! This is for happy people. Get it?

Douthat wraps it all up by arguing against Planned Parenthood's existence as the enemy of little girls' "sexual idealism" around the world. Those PP people are so—unbabylike. Unladylike! Does that rhyme? If they weren't depressed before, they sure will be after they read Ross's story.

I'm going to tell you a story about Ross himself, from his memoir, a tale from the days when he was not happy. He was in college at Harvard, at a party, where he met a tipsy, buxom blonde—he said she kinda looked like Reese Witherspoon. Reesey kissed Rossy, and laid bare her arousal. She even reassured him that she was on the Pill, so they could just go wild. You can imagine what happened. Ross went completely limp! He'd never been so turned off in his life. So scared. So *not happy!* Boy, did he learn a lesson. College boys everywhere can relate to that!

Ross became a Pentecostal during puberty—he wasn't born to it. His mom started following a faith healer 'cause she was really sick, and they prayed and prayed and prayed. It must've been really depressing, and sex wasn't even a part of it. It's quite the life story. Something went awry, though, 'cause the whole family stopped traveling the faith-healer circuit, and converted to Catholicism, the old-fashioned kind. You can just imagine how happy they all are now!

Ross's biography of profound religious conversion got under my skin, the one thing that made me just a teeny bit un-happy. You see, if the subject was *anything* other than sex in the New York Times, the editors would feel obliged to preface the op-ed by revealing the writer's religious agenda. Apparently, America's top-shelf publishers know so little about physiology, biology, and sexual history that their authors can just say *anything*, and it sticks, no matter how absurd.

Fact-checking? Not when it comes to fire and brimstone, baby! Let's not let "facts" get in the way of our moral imperatives. Don't fret your pretty little heads about what really happened in the "old days." My grandmothers and great-great-great grand-mothers got knocked up young, didn't always get hitched, and died in childbirth early—but that's so sad to think about, let's not dwell on it. Remember the good times, I say!

It must make Ross pout that unrelenting evidence proves ab-stinence programs are not only ineffective, they actually cause higher pregnancy rates than in places where young people have info and access to birth control. Eww! It can turn a smiley-face upside down if you're a Christian religious fanatic. But sometimes the truth is—proofy.

As for women having an infantile essential nature that desires innocence and vacuity above all other sexual traits, leading to an unparalleled state of happy brainlessness—gosh, how do you even begin to document that, outside of scripture and tattered Catholic catechism pamphlets?

Douthat's faith is based on the tenets of unapologetic misogyny, sexism, gender determinism, and an all-around "Father Knows Best" approach. I'm sure you've heard how well the Catholic clergy has led in this regard. In Christianity, men are the natural leaders, and must stand guard against their carnality. Grrr! Women must follow man, doting on him, caring for the hearth. Women have a lot to atone for, because they're the reason human beans got tossed out of the Garden of Eden. That's where God created everything in Seven Days and there was a Magic Apple and it tasted really good—which was premature and ill-advised. To say the least.

Now, in Catholicism—I was raised Catholic, brainwashed early—faith, sin, and hell are all anyone talks about! If you even *think* bad thoughts, that's as bad as doing them. Masturbation is really, really bad. Sex is so wrong, there's, like, a million ways to do it wrong and burn in hell forever. Only if you get in the missionary position and do it just to have babies, then it's OK. The Virgin Mary was happy, you know, 'cause she didn't have to go through all that sh*t. She was so full of grace.

Despite Ross's efforts, I have nagging questions that keep me from achieving my desired beatific state:

When will we stop allowing religious doctrine and its zealots from determining public policy on sexual health?

How long will these same people remain the arbiters of taste and convention in sexual relations?

Last I checked, George "God-Is-Speaking-Thru-Me" Bush is no longer the POTUS. The Christian religious right is not remotely the majority in this country. Why do we listen to them, over and over again, on the front pages of our country's most prestigious newspapers, preaching what's best for men, women, and children?

It's such a bummer. The perps who write these stories and lead these campaigns always seem to get revealed as disgusting closeted perverts. And I don't mean that in a happy way. How many more humiliations in the public square, starring avowedly chaste evangelicals, do we have to endure? It was bad enough reading about Ross's nausea at female flesh in college—I don't want to read the next chapter!

I'd like to see an atheist's op-ed on sex in the NYT, or even one from a recovering Catholic. I'd be happy, very happy to do it myself. Here's what I'd say:

Our cute little species desires both sexual familiarity and sexual variety. That's why we are so rarely monogamous over a lifetime, although we often enjoy its benefits for episodic periods. When unencumbered by religious shame, we feel perfectly fine about "having it all."

I'll use myself as an example! *Je ne regrette rien.* May I take a moment to thank all the lovers I've ever had for everything I learned from you? You-all are the best, and it makes my heart just want to burst with—oh, you know.

When young adults, past puberty, remain sexually inexperienced with their peers, it is because of dysfunction, not virtue. Something is wrong, and it's not happy. Sexual self-knowledge is a huge part—perhaps the biggest part—of growing up. Like taking your first steps, or speaking your first words, you gain enormous intelligence and independence every time you figure out another piece. You fall down and cry sometimes, but you can't wait to get back up. To learn that things are not black and white, to hold contradictions, ambiguity, and empathy in your body and mind at the same time: that's sexual maturity. You don't achieve it from cutting out paper dolls and keeping your knees crossed.

Fun clue: Men are sensitive creatures. They like to feel safe and adored, just like, you know—everyone else. Sometimes they don't always know what to do and don't feel like having the answer to everything.

And women? They can be total thrill-seekers; when they get sex on the brain, they'll get off with their fingers or their pet bunny or whatever else is around. They have brilliant ideas and can march into the battlefield with a double-sided ax.

It's dangerously stupid to talk about men and women as if they were different animals—when we have so much more in common, in our capacities, than we have differences. Hasn't everyone been a lot happier now that we no longer live our lives based on superstition? Why, at this point, do we ignore primary evidence—at our peril—and cling to shaming, stunted fairy tales?

I had a dream about Ross. He was eating an apple and he was happy. His mom got better and she didn't need him to take care of her anymore; she was happy, too. Men and women gathered around Ross and started kissing him. Tears ran down his cheeks. He was scared that everyone would find out, but the sexy happy people said, "No, Ross, it's okay, you're not crazy. You can have this, but you have to be honest about it, 'cause that's only fair."

And then Ross took a big giant bite.

Losing the Meatpacking District:
A Queer History of Leather Culture
Abby Tallmer

The recent history of Manhattan's Meatpacking District is a story about the homogenization of our city and the erasure of a generation of its people and their history. It is a story of how the intersecting forces of rising real estate prices, the Disneyfication of Times Square and Manhattan at large, the conservative national shift over the past two decades, and the onset of AIDS and the panic surrounding it have effectively eclipsed memories of a time when "Meatpacking District" was not a real-estate term.

Instead, the term was ironic shorthand for the patch of West Village blocks, centered roughly at 14th Street and Ninth Avenue, to which countless visitors flocked, seeking the alternative sexual universe that existed there before the invasion of slumming heterosexual tourists looking for Stella McCartney's latest couture designs.

At the height of the feminist, gay, and sexual revolutions of the 1960s and 70s through the mid-80s, the Meatpacking District was home to the city's thriving and mostly queer SM and sex club scene.

Far from being a desirable destination, the Far West Village, as it was known back then, was unknown territory to most New Yorkers except for butchers, neighborhood residents, and the select group of queer and kinky people who roamed the streets and filled the clubs there in the late-night hours, staggering home in the early morning as the sun was rising and most others were heading off to work. During the day, strong men dragged animal carcasses through the garbage-filled streets. It was an area reserved for those with iron stomachs, given the stench of dead flesh and rotting trash that permeated the air.

Growing up in the neighborhood, I was ashamed to invite my grade-school friends over for fear they would think I lived in a garbage dump. But at night, the place came alive and the unlit, otherwise desolate streets were filled with other men, also tough-looking, but clad in leather chaps and motorcycle jackets, with hankies protruding from their rear pockets and keys dangling from their sides. They lingered on street corners, purposefully eyeing one another, striking up conversations, offering each other a light, and often disappearing down mysterious alleyways or spilling through unmarked but much-trafficked doorways.

There were other characters as well—adventurous male/female couples; groups of nervous young gay men and women clearly new to the area and intent on a mission, often clad not in leather/fetish gear but in regular clothes; and the ever-present trans hookers, who were mostly black or Hispanic. Many of the hookers almost completely passed as women, as stunning as they were scantily dressed. They could often be seen awkwardly climbing into and out of the limos and trucks driven by the married men from Staten Island or New Jersey who traveled there just for them.

In the early 1970s, I lived five blocks north of Christopher Street and three blocks from the Hudson River. I was then about nine years old, a queer kid waiting for the right time to spring this news on my parents. I was raised in a very permissive household and often walked the streets alone even after dark. Needless to say, the night action in my neighborhood hardly went unnoticed by me and, in fact, served as the object of much curiosity.

I remember riding my bike around the neighborhood, making special trips past the piers and the bathhouses and through the deserted side streets west of Greenwich Street, and down 14th Street and the short blocks just below. Though I wasn't quite sure what exactly went on behind these hidden, locked doors, I knew somehow—God knows how—that whatever it was had to do with being gay, with being sexual, with a particular form of gay sexual expression that I gathered was in some way shameful. The very same men who cheerily said hi to me in my building's elevator usually looked more horrified than happy to see me when I greeted them from my bicycle as they loitered, regaled in leather, in alleyways or in front of dimly lit clubs or bathhouses.

As I would learn later, the unofficial center of all of this action was the "Triangle Building" on 14th Street and Ninth Avenue, which now houses Vento, a popular Italian restaurant opened in 2004, but was then the site of some of the most notorious leather bars in the city. Entrances to a stunning array of SM and sex clubs and backrooms lined both the Eighth and the Ninth Avenue sides of the Triangle. Those directly on the Triangle included the nationally known Hellfire Club, the Vault, J's, The Man Hole, and many others.

Queer clubs within strolling distance included the notorious

Mineshaft, the Anvil, the Asstrick, the Cellblock, the International Stud, the Glory Hole, and, later, the Lure. Patrons migrated between them all night long, every night of the week, back when sexual freedom defined an era.

Nearly all of these clubs, except the Hellfire Club and the Vault, were predominantly gay, though a few stray women could be spotted here and there in some of the less strict men's clubs. The Mineshaft's door policy, however, was notoriously strict, and many gay men were turned away each night for violating its strict leather/macho dress code. That didn't keep some inventive women from testing whether it was foolproof.

I know this to be true firsthand, for one night just after I turned 18, my best friends, Saul and Brian, decided that it would be fun to dress me up and sneak me into the Mineshaft with them. As I am rather the femme type of lesbian, I was terrified about passing the rigid door inspection, but the boys picked out my outfit—white T-shirt, black leather jacket, jeans, and boots, with a sock in my pants prominently displaying package—and did my hair expertly; they even gave me a fake five o'clock shadow. I remember shuffling in line behind Brian and ahead of Saul— I pleaded to be last, but Brian said this would look suspicious—and I vividly remember trying not to stare at the floor too obviously as the doorman inspected my ID. After what seemed like forever but was undoubtedly a matter of seconds, the doorman muttered, "Next" and that was it. I was in. But poor Saul, who stood behind me in line, was barred at the door because there was something "too effeminate" about him.

Inside, I remember seeing a sea of nude, half-nude, harnessed and chained male bodies (the bottoms) and muscular men in full leather (the tops) in groups of three, or four, or two, or eight, or more. Some of the tops held whips and paddles of various sorts, and many were noisily using them on their willing victims.

I remember all sorts of sounds: from the bottoms, cries and whimpers and gasps and moans and shrill but insincere pleas of "Stop!," tops barking orders at their slaves sternly or angrily or calmly, while others yelled numbers for their subjects to repeat, or let out long strings of outrageously profane, usually effeminizing, epithets, or simply emitted guttural, primal groans. All the collective words and sighs were punctuated by the unmistakable sounds of flagellation—wooden paddles striking flesh, the snapping of bullwhips slicing through the air and landing sharply on human targets, the ringing of bare hands making contact with buttocks. I stood there transfixed, thinking, *This is what men do when women aren't around.*

I was sure from the moment I entered that I wouldn't be able to stay long before being found out, so I was determined to take it all in. But my secret was never discovered. After a half hour we reluctantly left to rejoin Saul.

This adventure took place a full year or two before I discovered the Lesbian Sex Mafia (LSM), New York's first and only lesbian SM organization, founded in 1981. I came upon the group just as I was growing convinced that no network existed for women who were interested in exploring SM with other women.

Which brings us back to the Mineshaft. The immediate and intense exhilaration I felt upon getting past the guard and into the main play area came from the liberating realization that not one of the men in that room cared about me—the real me, not the sock-down-my-pants me. I'm sure the overpowering smell of God knows how many bottles of poppers had something to do with this feeling, too.

Even as a woman, I experienced the Mineshaft as my first purely queer sexual space. The club imparted a feeling of immense optimism, opportunity, safety, and community. If you were gay and in the Mineshaft or any of the other queer SM clubs in the Meatpacking District in the 1970s, 80s, and into the early 90s, you felt, often for the first time in your life, completely removed, divorced, immune from socially imposed heterosexual judgment.

Fortunately, a few years later I was able to capture a similar feeling in a purely lesbian sexual space when LSM co-founder Jo A. began hosting Ms. Trick, a series of women-only SM nights at the otherwise gay male Asstrick Club.

These queer SM clubs gave us a place to feel that we were no longer outsiders—or rather, they made us feel that it was better to be outsiders, together, than to force ourselves to be like everybody else. This was long before our self-appointed gay leaders began telling us that getting married was every queer person's highest goal—though certainly then, as now, there were many extralegal long-term gay couples happily living together.

Back then, many of us believed that gay liberation was rooted in sexual liberation, and we believed that liberation was rooted in the right—no, the need—to claim ownership of our bodies, to experience and celebrate sexuality in as many forms as possible, limited only by our time and imagination. We believed that gay pride was impossible without sexual pride, including leather pride. Though we did not know it then, in the Meatpacking District of the 1970s through the early 90s, we were living in one of the most permissive times in modern history and in one of the most permissive places in modern history.

Today, when I try to explain this history to younger queers, they often don't believe me. The Meatpacking District during that period has attained an almost mythological status for younger members of the LGBT community that makes it impossible for them to believe the concrete reality many of us took for granted back then. We were kids then, in terms of our experience and the sense of possibility we felt. We fully expected that being gay would only get better and easier as we got older. Ours was the first generation to celebrate and experience our sexuality in all its alternative forms—and that we did as much as possible. Most of us never foresaw a more restrictive world and never imagined that our joyful experiment would end. Little did we know that many of us would never live to adulthood, that this moment would be gone in a flash, and that an era would vanish with it.

Never take your present for granted, because there's no telling how quickly and how thoroughly it will be erased.

Penis Gagging, BDSM, and Rape Fantasy:
The Truth About Kinky Sexting
Rachel Kramer Bussel

"You don't want to gag a woman with your penis unless you have some serious issues with the way you see women." So says Kirsten Powers, ex-girlfriend of sex-scandal star Congressman Anthony Weiner, in a piece for The Daily Beast. She is referencing his sexting relationship with a Las Vegas blackjack dealer, which made national headlines. The transcript of their texts was posted by Radar Online, including one bit that prompted Powers's musing: "You will gag on me before you c★★ with me in you" and "[I'm] thinking about gagging your hot mouth with my c★★★."

This article is not about Weiner. I'm pretty much over political sex scandals and inclined to think that someone like Weiner wants to get caught, consciously or unconsciously. The only positive thing I can say about such scandals is that they do help shed light on just how unenlightened we are about topics like monogamy and BDSM. Powers is an example of a woman making a blanket statement about something she clearly doesn't know the first thing about, simply because it offends her.

You know the phrase "Taken out of context, I must seem so strange?" That goes double for pulling random bits of erotic conversation, texted or otherwise, and analyzing them as if they told a whole story. Without the motivation of the person sending and receiving them, you really don't know anything, and yet a default anti–BDSM reaction seems to be acceptable. Our public squeamishness over the fact that some people can eroticize pain, degradation, and being ordered around, safely, consensually, and pleasurably, is nothing more than a prejudice that needs to be eradicated.

For instance, I had an extended kinky relationship with someone where the bulk of our exchanges occurred via email, phone calls, and texting; only a minority of our interactions were in person. We had built up plenty of previous knowledge about each other when he texted me, "I want to rape you." Now, of course, if someone had grabbed my phone at that very moment and that was all they saw, they might think this person was violent. But there is a world of difference between discussing a rape fantasy and actual rape; a person saying they want to gag another person (or be gagged) would, in a consensual case, mean that both parties are mutually interested in the exchange. I knew exactly what he meant, and he knew that I knew—and that I thought it was hot. That's not something I'd take lightly, and I'll admit that even though we'd been talking about that very thing, using the words *force* and *make* were easier for me than using the word *rape*. The truth is, we went farther in some ways than I ever have with a lover precisely because I trusted him so much, and because our fantasies aligned so perfectly, feeding off each other.

I'm aware that from afar it might be hard to tell the difference when all you have is someone's words, stark and disconnected—which is why I wouldn't presume to jump in and tell someone else how to behave, or how to fantasize. I can tell you that when I read Powers's words, I felt slut-shamed, because I've had exchanges just as risqué, just as perverted (and I use that word proudly). The art of verbal degradation is a fine one, and it's not for the fainthearted or those who have poor social skills or misogynists or those who simply want to spout out their fantasy without acknowledging the other person.

Another lover, with whom I'd engaged in rough sex, straight-out asked me how far was too far, what names I liked to be called, thereby both establishing some boundaries and, in my opinion, making for some hot foreplay. Far from detracting from a dominant's power, checking in, as well as making a submissive acknowledge exactly what it is that floats their boat, can be very hot.

Again, I am not talking about nonconsensual exchanges. But I think it's important for those of us who are kinky, or who have engaged in kinky play, to stand up for our right to do so. That doesn't mean you have to post the highly personal details of your exchanges online, and I wouldn't recommend running for office and leaving a paper trail of things you wouldn't want your constituents to know, but it does mean speaking up for yourself and not letting ignorance rule. It also means checking our own inner censors and making sure we don't turn around and make unwarranted judgments about other people's sex lives, especially where we don't have all the facts.

Please note that I'm not saying anyone has to participate in BDSM or even fully understand it; I'm all about keeping a live-and-let-live attitude. But when having an opinion about a specific case morphs into having an opinion about anyone, anywhere, who might be into the kind of sexual fantasy that you're not, you need to step back and analyze how your own prejudices come into play.

The point of fantasies is that they come from somewhere that isn't always logical or rational. Some people might be inclined to investigate where their fantasies come from, what they "mean," but I tend to think of them the way I think of art, where there are multiple interpretations, where the point is to make us feel something stemming from somewhere beyond our brain. To me, that's what makes fantasies hot, and it makes me quite certain that my brain is my biggest sex organ and that someone's filthy mind will likely impress me more quickly than any other body part.

Drawing a direct, judgmental line, as Powers does, between a fantasy expressed consensually between adults and one's own politics and interests should be offensive no matter what you think of Weiner or BDSM. Maybe it's not for you, and that's perfectly fine, but that doesn't mean it's wrong for everyone, and I'd hate to live in a world where someone else reigned supreme and told me what I could and couldn't do in bed, or on my phone. It's all too easy to sound morally superior when you are personally put off by some behavior, especially something sexual, without ever considering that others could be equally justified in being outraged about your personal peccadilloes. So for all of us who are into things like gagging, choking, and giving or following orders, don't let anyone tell you that you have a problem. I'm not assessing your sex life, or your psyche, so please don't make sweeping judgments about mine. Anthony Weiner may or may not have issues with women. He's certainly not alone in what he fantasizes about, but the only assumption you can make from what he texted is that he's into sending dirty, kinky texts. And there's nothing wrong with that!

Adrian's Penis: Care and Handling
Adrian Colesberry

Adrian's penis has many manually operated functions and is designed for people who like to engage with a penis. Maybe that makes it seem like a lot of trouble, but if you think your snatch is some low-maintenance dream, you're operating under a delusion. It might help you adopt the proper attitude if you think about Adrian's penis the same way he thinks about your ass. Stop thinking of it as *his* penis and start thinking of it as *your* penis. Not yours in a trivial capitalist sense, like it's property, but more like it's a field of beans that a farmer has planted right behind her house. She cares for the field all year long. She knows when to feed and water it, when to work the field, and when to let it rest. In the following, find instructions on how to feed, water, work, and rest Adrian's penis.

Adrian's Shy Erection

Sexually demanding reader, please don't envision a constantly floppy Adrian Colesberry daily inventing new excuses for his defective arousal mechanism. Aside from occasionally being knocked out by drink, his cock has proven reliable over the years with two exceptions: in the getting-to-know-you part of the relationship and again when the relationship is going badly.[1]

A typical first time with Adrian Colesberry plays out like a physical comedy routine where every time the thirsty heroine bends down to the water fountain, the stream retreats to a dribble. He'll go down on you until he gets his erection, but he'll lose it as soon as he reaches for the condom. If you're kind enough, you'll get him hard again in your hand or mouth, but right when he tears open the condom, he'll go all floppy again.

You may be perfectly willing to keep sucking his cock, and while your generosity will be more than welcome, it'll just make Adrian feel weird after a bit to be in your mouth without getting hard enough fast enough.

> *Tip:* When Adrian is having his first-time erection problems, there is such a thing as paying too much attention to his cock.

The generous reader might have been looking forward to sucking Adrian's flaccid penis to erection. But not knowing how to judge whether he's getting "hard enough fast enough," how will you know when to abandon your project of making him hard in your mouth? You needn't be concerned about the timing. Adrian will remove his cock from your mouth if he's getting self-conscious and switch you to another activity. Another activity means, of course, more pussy-eating. As long as his shy erection is in town, he'll eat your pussy until his tongue cramps up completely and even his neck, where all the tongue muscles are attached.

The sensitive reader may be overly worried about what exactly to do when Adrian's shy erection shows up. Don't be. You can do anything that makes you feel like you're helping out, because Adrian's erection problems will go away on your second or third time regardless of what you do.[2]

Your cure for Adrian's shy erection is like your mom's cure for a cold. A cold cures itself, but your mom wants to feel like she's doing something to take care of you, so she makes you soup or gives you a pill, and when you get better she feels like she had a part in it. In the same way, do whatever you like to help fix Adrian's shy erection and when a few days later he's fucking your brains out, you'll feel like you had something to do with it. Throw a penny into a fire, light incense in an abalone shell, masturbate for him, read him French poetry. It'll all work.

And remember, while you wait for his penis to come on-line, someone who combines the desperate enthusiasm of a 16-year-old boy with the know-how of a grown man will be munching on your box for hours. Assuming you enjoy cunnilingus, everything will work out just fine.

Adrian's Reluctant Orgasm
It takes a long time for Adrian to come with a woman; always has. It can't be a physical thing, because he comes easily when he's masturbating.

But it will be several weeks or months into your relationship before he has an orgasm with you. The experienced reader may be hearing this with a shake of the head: "Adrian won't last two minutes with me. There's this thing I do with my tongue/ finger/ vagina…" Perhaps, but read on.

Best that can be figured, Adrian's overactive orgasm suppression mechanism got Frankensteined together when the standard propaganda about how a man has to last forever in the sack grafted itself onto his trained-from-the-womb perfectionism. Whenever he did anything, like take a shit or recite a multiplication table or bring home a piece of child-art made from paste and pinto beans, his mother would say, "Little Adrian, you're just perfect." He knew it wasn't true, but in an effort not to disappoint the kindly woman who'd brought him into this world, he did his best to keep up the front by behaving the way he thought a perfect person would behave.

It's Baby Adrian who puts the brakes on when he gets close to orgasm. "What are you doing, Adrian? We're not supposed to come."

Adrian tries to explain, "It's only at first that we're not supposed to."

"How are we going to last forever if you come?"

"It's not literally *forever*."

"I've heard it's forever."

"She already came. That's why we went down on her for so long. Now we can go ahead."

"That's not how I understood it."

Then Adrian gets all mad, like, "That's because you're what? Six?! You don't understand anything. Just let me come!" But by this time the window of opportunity has closed again.

It's not that he doesn't get close. He can come easily in the first 30 seconds. But he always holds back because he doesn't want to prematurely ejaculate. That would make him a premature ejaculator.

Plus, he doesn't want to stop having sex so soon after starting. On taking the first bite of his favorite meal, his next thought after

That's delicious! is not *Gee, I hope this experience ends immediately.*

A ways after that first one, a second window of opportunity opens, but by the time he recognizes it, an automatic part of his brain has already taken over and stifled his orgasm again. And so it goes with the third window and the fourth.[3]

The cynical reader might suspect that this up-to-now objective account of how to make love to Adrian Colesberry has been corrupted by a crass attempt to promote Adrian Colesberry's sexual athleticism, that this complaint about his not being able to come is obviously meant to imply that his lovemaking will be lengthy, and that the next chapter will be an equally transparent moan about the inconvenient girthiness of his cock. Not at all!

Adrian holds no delusions about women wanting a man to last forever. In his experience, they resoundingly haven't. It's great for those first few times when you just can't get enough of each other, but after that, if you are anything like every woman he's ever been with, you'll be over it. Following the zero, one, or several orgasms you want to have, Adrian's erection turns from a fun new toy into a party guest who won't leave at the end of the evening. "Oh, that's still there. Do I have to do something about it?"

The answer is an emphatic no. You don't have to do anything about it. Adrian enjoys fucking more than coming. If he just wants to come, he won't bother fucking you in the first place; he'll jerk off. So just call "Time" when you're done and he's all good.

In Adrian's experience, the trickiest part of his not coming will be managing your frustration. If you're accustomed to having the power to bring off a man with your hand, mouth, or vagina, the discovery that you don't have your finger on the trigger of Adrian Colesberry might not make you happy.[4]

The sensitive reader may perceive a profound ungenerousness or distancing mechanism in Adrian's not achieving the ultimate sexual pleasure. You may read his never coming as *I don't really need you.* Please do not indulge this train of thought. If Adrian is fucking you, he needs you.

Endnotes

1 There have been two times in Adrian's life when his shy erection has not been a temporary, up-front problem: with the Wife and once before that with the Deliberate One. We can breeze over the Wife by assuming that you won't force Adrian exclusively into the roles of father figure, caretaker, doctor, and provider, not leaving any part for his penis to play because Adrian the father-caretaker-doctor-provider will not fuck his child-invalid-patient-ward.

The Deliberate One offers a far more instructive example of how Adrian's erection can be driven into hibernation. She lived at the women's dorm where Adrian was a waiter in college. He became part of her drinking circle and ended up with a little bit of a crush on her, which grew into a lot of a bit of a crush once he learned that her main goal in college, aside from graduating of course, was to fuck at least one person other than her high school boyfriend, who was the man she'd given her virginity to and the man she planned to marry after college. A noble cause. Needless to say, Adrian wanted to sign up.

Tip: Historically speaking, people have underexploited the ability to help themselves reach their potential by fucking Adrian Colesberry. If you have any life goals that he can help along in this way, please let him know.

Adrian soon learned from another girl in their circle that the Deliberate One had chosen him to do the fucking. So with no fear of rejection, he asked her out. For their first few dates they just necked in his car, but eventually he got her over to his place and before the evening was done, she let him take her pants off. He went down on her for a long time, using everything he'd learned between the Loved One's legs. When he came up for air, she lay back in anticipation of his entry. And that was when he lost his erection. At that moment, he could have said truthfully, for the first and the last time, "I swear, this has never happened to me before." He felt sure that the problem would pass, but it didn't. Weeks went by and they were only ever about boob handling and eating pussy.

Unless your fantasy affair with Adrian Colesberry involves him going down on you and a lot of making out, he's apparently not the greatest guy to fuck around with on your boyfriend or husband. On the other hand, he's older now, of course, and the Deliberate One is not you, needless to say. So maybe Adrian and, more important, Adrian's penis, would be thrilled to be one-half of the adulterous affair you'd like to have behind the back of your lucky someone. Just don't put a down payment on a condo/love nest until you test-drive his cock for a bit.

Knowing how much she wanted to fuck someone else, Adrian felt really guilty about not being able to get it up for her. It was as if a terminal cancer patient had asked him to give her a fuck before dying, but he couldn't because of his ridiculous, uncooperative erection. Then it dawned on him that maybe she could do something to make it more cooperative. In his first-ever attempt at asking anyone to do him a favor in bed, he asked her if she had ever considered sucking his cock. She had, so that was good, but she said she only did that for her boyfriend. Afterward, he no longer felt guilty about not being able to fuck her.

Depending on your perspective, Adrian's impotence in this case was triggered either by a respectful objection to the Deliberate One's infidelity or by her lack of physical attention. The monogamous, blow job–averse reader should choose to believe that Adrian's sense of rectitude kept his penis flaccid; the adulterous reader should choose to believe that he's one enthusiastic blow job away from getting hard enough to fuck the pope's girlfriend.

2   Despite her name or maybe because of it, the Great One did make the beautiful mistake of sucking Adrian's cock for an uncomfortably long time in an attempt to solve his initial shy erection. His problems lasted a particularly short time with the Innocent One, who never once touched Adrian's shy erection. No credit to her, though; she barely touched his penis at all, shy or otherwise. The Last One more deliberately ignored the early erection difficulties, to the extent that when he mentioned it, she didn't even speak, as if she hadn't heard him. Good move.

The Talker, from back in college, and the Expert had the most hysterical responses to his shy erection. The Talker imagined that his erection was flagging due to a lack of kink and flipped into every conceivable sexual position to inspire him. Eighteen years later, the Expert also chose to up the kink: after an abortive bout of doggie style, she did an acrobatic maneuver where she ended up with her legs wrapped around his neck, putting them into a standing 69 where she deepthroated him. That worked for a bit, but when she came up for air, Adrian still didn't have enough to pull a condom over.

At this point, the Expert spun into a total panic. Her alarm grew and grew until she blurted out, "I'm going to ask my mom for one of dad's pills." Apparently, her father took an erection pill to get hard.

Adrian started to tell her for the one-millionth time that his penis would work OK soon enough, but she looked utterly lost at having failed to generate a hard cock in the way that she was used to. So he changed his mind and said, "Fantastic. Definitely ask your mother."

He felt quite generous about his assent. Not only did it make the Expert happy but it'd give dad a thrill to hear that some young stud, relatively speaking, needed a bit of the same chemical assistance that he needed himself. Mainly, though, he wanted to hear the Expert report on the conversation where she asked her mother for one of her husband's pills. "Thanks for the hard-on pills, Mom. Keep 'em coming, and this guy you've never met can pork your daughter." Words every girl's mother dreams of hearing.

Moving from the absurd to the sublime, the prize-winning responses to Adrian's early loss of erection belong to the Enthusiast and the Kind One: When Adrian fell to half mast, The Enthusiast would lie down beside him, cup his balls in one hand, and, with her other hand, masturbate herself. To break down why this is so brilliant, grabbing his balls maintained contact with his naughty bits, but not a part that needed to do anything, so he couldn't interpret her touch as a demand of any kind. And the masturbation communicated that she hadn't taken their forced break as a failure. She was going to be sexually satisfied whether he fucked her or not. That made him feel a lot better.

The Kind One pulled a maneuver of even greater genius, if you can imagine it. At his first failure, she jumped off the bed, grabbed some lotion from the bedside table, and gave him a foot massage. Saying, without saying, *I'm going to love you whether your penis is on board or not.* Not only was this the kindest maneuver, but it got the quickest result.

3 The only person to break Adrian's reluctant orgasm was the First One. It remains controversial what exactly caused his orgasm to flip from reluctant to nearly immediate. All the evidence for all points of view will be presented here in a balanced way so that you can make up your own mind.

Once she decided that they were an item, Adrian became the beneficiary of the First One's girlfriend ethics:

- *The primary rule:* Any time she found Adrian with a hard-on, it was her job to make it go away.
- *The secondary rule:* She was responsible for harvesting all his semen.

The lawyerly reader might object that the secondary rule is simply a corollary of the primary. But although the primary rule provides the foundation for the second, it is not a sufficient condition. The primary rule only required that she solved the erections that she found. The secondary rule required her to be there to find all his erections, something she did with near perfect fidelity. Often at great inconvenience to herself, she would spend every night with Adrian. He thought at first that she was doing all this on account of a deep affection, but really it was an ethical imperative, as follows:

The First One is Adrian's girlfriend iff the First One harvests all Adrian's Semen.

The First One harvests all Adrian's Semen iff the First One sleeps over every night.

The First One sleeps over every night.

QED

[Where iff = if and only if, in other words the singular sufficient condition(s).]

At night, she'd get there just before he went to bed and they'd fuck until he came. Then they'd sleep until his second erection woke up one of them at around three in the morning; then they'd fuck again. Then she'd take care of his morning erection, of course, after which she'd promptly leave for work.

This pattern wasn't immediately established. His reluctant orgasm heroically persisted for several weeks before he came for the first time, but once she'd gotten her foot in the door, she had him coming progressively quicker. Within two weeks, he'd stopped masturbating altogether because she was keeping up with his testicles' production capacity. Adrian, as you can imagine, felt a bit confused and unmanned by the arrangement. He was hardly lasting forever as he knew he should be. But the First One's positive attitude, driven by her high level of girlfriend accomplishment as defined by her own ethics, convinced him that everything was OK.

Besides, she would already have had an orgasm by the time she tucked his cock inside her, since she came beforehand by humping his thigh, so Adrian ultimately was able to cast a positive light on lasting barely three minutes inside her: he hadn't begun to prematurely ejaculate. *Not at all!* What he'd done was custom-develop a hyperefficient style of lovemaking. Fucking was pointless for her since she could only have clitoral orgasms. So in his genius, he'd cut it down to a bare minimum.

The first theory to explain his unusual behavior is called the Masturbation Substitution Theory. It holds that if you (or anyone) were to arrange your life such that you're ready and willing to fuck as frequently as Adrian would masturbate, he'd ultimately make the switch and fuck you in place of masturbating, which would automatically endow your lovemaking with the ejaculatory efficiency of his masturbation.

This conventional explanation faces a challenge from the Mononucleosis Hypothesis. Some have correctly pointed out that, halfway through the relationship, Adrian contracted mononucleosis from the First One. Theory holds that the catastrophic impact on his immune system had the side effect of making him a premature ejaculator.

The curious reader, if annoyed at how Adrian rarely comes, could stage an experiment. First try harvesting all his semen and then infect him with a virus—nothing too serious, please—and see which technique makes him ejaculate faster.

4 After he'd gone to all that trouble using the 69 to finesse the Loved One into giving him head, Adrian found her fellatio disappointingly tepid. One night, lying there with his cock in her barely animated mouth, everything became crystal clear to him: Her old boyfriend had shot off in her mouth without warning and she thought that was going to happen with Adrian, too, bringing their fun to an end. He thought, Good news! I can clear up this misunderstanding in a jiffy!

Raising his head off the mattress, he happily announced, "You know there's no way I'm ever going to come in your mouth, so you don't have to worry about that at all!" Now he figured she could relax and enjoy sucking his cock as much as he enjoyed eating her pussy, but instead of the reassurance he had intended, she took his statement as a mortal insult against her cocksucking skills. She heard "You give head so lousy that you could stay down there till next Tuesday and I'd never get off."

In response to his unintended challenge, the Loved One pushed her cocksucking to heights of hair-raising intensity. She encouraged him to ejaculate in her mouth, even before he'd fucked her. "I've got a washcloth right here!" After dishing out several servings of the best blow job that came out of her kitchen, she got positively panicky about getting him off. To give her some hope to hang on to, he abandoned the position that busting his nut during head would be impossible and took to promising that he was seriously getting very close to getting off.

A few weeks into the Loved One's blow job ejaculation project, Adrian finally came while fucking her. He was so surprised that he completely forgot what they'd been going through and reverted to being worried that he'd come too soon. "Were you done?!" he asked. She gave him a look like, *Yeah, I was done two months ago.*

The Continuing Criminalization of Teen Sex
Ellen Friedrichs

Sometimes it seems as if we live in a world that is getting more fearful about teens by the day. But while the specific concerns may be new, targeting youth really isn't. Since the dawn of recorded history, adolescents have caused adults a fair amount of stress, even as the sources of that stress have changed from generation to generation. Today, people seem to be worried about sexting and self-injury, teen moms and bi-curiosity. A few years back, it was school shootings, the oral sex epidemic, and methamphetamine. When I was growing up in the late 80s and early 90s, AIDS was on everyone's mind, and the panic over heavy metal music (does it lead to Satanism? Murder? Suicide? Too much black eye makeup?) was just calming down. Ten years earlier, alarm bells had sounded about young runaways. Before that, it was hippies, potheads, and free love. That followed fears about hoodlums, the homosexual menace, and teen marriage, which only appeared after anxiety about flappers and girls who wanted to ride bicycles in short new haircuts subsided. Indeed, adult nervousness about teens has always run the gambit. But while we fret over just about everything, the idea of minors having sex seems to elicit a unique brand of paranoia, and these days this paranoia has convinced a surprising number of people that an ever expanding list of sexual experiences should actually be prosecutable offenses when they involve minors.

This view is a demonstrated shift from the recent past. When I was in high school 20 years ago, most kids weren't worried that the long arm of the law would reach into their highly personal, and obviously juvenile, sexual encounters (though gay boys, and black boys who dated white girls, have always had to look over their shoulders). And usually, this was for the best. Personally, I'm pretty sure that my rocky road to adulthood would not have been any smoother had the authorities discovered the revealing Polaroids that my 14-year-old girlfriends and I took of ourselves at a sleepover. Or had my 17-year-old boyfriend (a fellow who, if Facebook is to be believed, is now a happily married father of two) been charged with the crime of statutory rape when we had sex the following year. But things have changed over the past two decades, and we are currently living in a society with a legal system that can lump pedophiles together with teenagers having sex, that can treat kids who text naked pictures of themselves to a classmate the same way it treats child pornographers.

This change has occurred for a few reasons. One is that we are at a crossroads where old laws are meeting new technology with sometimes catastrophic collisions. Another is that over the past 15 years there has been an increase in the enforcement of statutory rape laws. These are laws that ban persons over the age of consent (which is different in every state) from having sex with anyone under the age of consent. In cases of statutory rape it is usually understood that a teen has agreed to have sex, but this agreement isn't considered valid since juveniles are regarded as too young to make such a decision. Statutory rape is different from child molestation, where an adult is typically charged with abusing a prepubescent child. It is also legally different from sexual assault or forcible rape. The word *rape* is used in this situation because it is assumed that pressure or coercion must be involved when there is a difference in age between sex partners. To be sure, statutory rape laws can be an important tool in preventing sexual manipulation of teens by adults. But they can also punish kids involved in noncoercive situations—for example, a teen over the age of consent who has sex with a peer who is underage.

Today, most states set the age of consent at 16 to 18. This is a lot higher than it was a century ago, when 10 or 12 was the norm (though in the case of Delaware it was seven!). Moral reformers of the day, already fighting for temperance, suffrage, and social purity, successfully advocated to raise the age, and by the 1920s the age of consent for heterosexual sex was increased in almost all 48 states. But while they have been on the books for well over a hundred years, prohibitions against statutory rape began to be implemented more frequently in the late 1990s. Oddly, this was a result of the passage of the 1996 Welfare Reform Act, which was designed to reduce the number of people receiving welfare payments. One way the bill sought to do so was by decreasing the number of "welfare moms"—basically single women with children who received social assistance. At the time, these women were a big target, often finding themselves blamed for draining welfare funds and cheating the system. In 1993, President Bill Clinton even championed the Welfare Reform Act with the claim that reducing welfare benefits "would be some incentive for people not to have dependent children out of wedlock."

It was in this climate that a study emerged showing that the majority of teen moms were not having babies with the boys from their geometry class. Rather, the research demonstrated, it was men in their twenties who were most likely to blame for underage pregnancies. So in addition to all its other money-saving strategies, the Welfare Reform Act encouraged states to, "aggressively enforce statutory rape laws" as a way to prevent young single mothers from draining the system. This aggressive enforcement has remained in many places long after the hysteria over welfare cheats has died down.

One unintended result of the increased prosecutions has been the criminalizing of teens most people wouldn't label as sexual abusers. Take Genarlow Wilson, for example. Wilson served three years in a Georgia prison after a conviction stemming from a 2005 New Year's Eve party where the then 17-year-old boy received oral sex from a 15-year-old girl. Another kid took a picture of the act, that kid's parents found the camera, the police were notified, and Wilson was arrested. Neither the girl in the photos nor her parents wanted to press charges. And despite the fact that Wilson was only two years older, he was above the age of consent in Georgia and she was below it. At the time, Georgia had a mandatory minimum sentence of 10 years for this crime. So that's what he got—10 years in jail for getting a blow job. A year into his sentence, the law was changed to make the maximum penalty in this situation a still pretty serious 12 months in jail. Even so, it took another two years for a judge to allow Wilson's release, and the boy was locked up longer than many serious felons.

Photographic proof is, of course, far from the only trigger of a statutory rape charge for a teenager. Charges often arise after parents notify the police about an incident. The result can be law enforcement that relates more to individual parental anger than it does to the gravity of the crime allegedly committed. Arrests can also come about as the result of state laws mandating that doctors, therapists, teachers, and even parents report *any* teen sexual activity that they get wind of.

One boy who found himself shouldering the burden of a sex offender conviction as a result of such snitching was a 16-year-old from Iowa named Ricky Blackman. Blackman became known to the authorities after a 13-year-old girl he met at a club for teens told her social worker that the two had had consensual sex. Because he was over the age of consent in that state and the girl was under it, Blackman was charged and convicted as a sex offender. This status meant that the boy was removed from his high school and prohibited from being in the presence of children other than his younger brother. He couldn't go near schools, day-care centers, or parks. His 11-year-old brother couldn't bring friends into their house. If his younger brother had been a girl, the teen would have been removed from his home altogether. To really drive home the point that Blackman was a danger to society, his driver's license had the phrase "sex offender" stamped in red letters under his photo. His mother, Mary Duval—whose tireless advocacy on his behalf eventually helped secure his release from the registry— told a Nevada news station that sex offender registries are "setting registered offenders up for failure."

In other situations, teens find themselves in a legal bind once a high-profile case captures the public's attention. When, in 2007, 16-year-old Jamie Lynn Spears, then a teen actor starring in a Disney show, announced that she was pregnant by her 18-year-old boyfriend, Casey Aldridge, there was speculation that the boy would be charged with statutory rape. But no one could quite figure out where she actually got pregnant. Spears split her time between her home in Louisiana, which had one set of laws, and the set of her TV show in California, which had another. It was soon discovered that Aldridge was not quite two years older than Spears. This meant he could have been charged in California, but not in Louisiana. That is because Louisiana is one of 11 states with close-in-age or "Romeo and Juliet" laws on the books. These laws ensure that if a couple is close in age (typically between two and three years apart), even if one person is over the age of consent, then the case is looked at differently than if a 25-year-old had sex with a 15-year-old. Nevertheless, despite the fact that California does not have this legal loophole, prosecutors there declined to pursue the case.

That wasn't the initial decision in another high-profile case. In September 2010, Massachusetts teens Sean Mulveyhill, 17, and Austin Renaud, 18, were charged with statutory rape for having sex with a 15-year-old girl named Phoebe Prince. Prince made national headlines after committing suicide in the face of relentless bullying, and there were calls for something to be done. Since Massachusetts had no anti-bullying laws, the DA went for something that was indeed illegal: statutory rape—despite the determination early on in the investigation that the girl took her life after suffering from relentless harassment, not as a result of her sexual relationships. And though the boys she slept with seemed to be members of the social circle that was intent on tormenting her, they did not appear to be the bullying ringleaders. But in bringing statutory rape charges in this way—for a purpose unrelated to the harm done by the sexual encounter—the DA continued the national trend of inconsistently and haphazardly applying such laws. Ultimately, the following May, after a request from Prince's family, the charges were dropped. Still, the fact that the charges were brought in the first place served as harsh warning for all teens.

The history of how statutory rape laws and age-of-consent rules have been applied to same-sex couples is somewhat different. While lesbians were rarely considered by lawmakers, many states passed unique prohibitions against sex between men. Often these laws imposed far harsher penalties for same-sex statutory rape cases than they did in comparable situations between opposite-sex partners. One of the most famous victims of this disparity was a developmentally delayed teen named Matthew Limon. In 2000, Limon was living in a group home in Kansas. A week after his 18th birthday, the boy performed oral sex on another boy who was 14 at the time. Both teens said the sex was consensual. But because Kansas had sodomy laws that applied only to gay men, and because Limon was legally an adult while the other boy was a minor, he was convicted of sodomy and sentenced to 17 years in jail. Had he performed oral sex on a 14-year-old girl, the maximum sentence would have been just 15 months. Limon spent five and a half years in jail before finally being released in 2005. His freedom was not won due to the compassion of the system, but rather as a by-product of *Lawrence v. Texas*, the 2003 case that saw the repeal of the federal sodomy prohibitions. Once those laws were overturned, Kansas and other states were forced to strike down laws that punished underage sex more severely if it involved homosexual acts.

Yet despite the fact that the federal sodomy laws were over-turned, some states still try to criminalize gay sex. One way is by keeping the invalidated sodomy laws on the books, in case the Supreme Court reverses its earlier decision. If that occurs, the state won't have to try to pass new laws criminalizing sodomy. Additionally, eight states still have what are called *crimes against nature* laws. These laws make it a crime to have sex that is not considered "natural." So what isn't natural? Well, bestiality and necrophilia are usually on the list. But, often, so are homosexual sex acts, anal sex, and occasionally even oral sex. Though most states understood that crimes against nature laws were invalidated by the passage of *Lawrence v. Texas*, eight states apparently did not. The result is that despite the fact that there are no longer laws that officially make it a crime to have sex with the same sex, some states still try to prosecute gay men and boys for doing so.

There are also, of course, situations where girls are labeled criminals for having sex. One girl, a Georgian named Wendy Whitaker, spent 12 years as a registered sex offender. The crime that got her there? Shortly after turning 17 she performed one act of oral sex on a boy in her class. It was a few weeks before the boy's 16th birthday, and because she was legally over the age of consent and he was under it, Whitaker was convicted of sodomy and required to register as a sex offender. This designation, and all the accompanying residency, work, and social restrictions, remained with her until September 2010, when a federal lawsuit allowed a few select sex offenders, including Whitaker, to petition a Superior Court judge to gain their release from the registry.

Needless to say, the most common reason girls find themselves facing sex-related charges is not because they have had consensual sex with a younger teen. Rather, most young female sex offenders bear this label after being arrested for prostitution. Despite the fact that it is against the law for an adult to have sex with anyone under the age of consent, if there is an exchange of money—even if it is money that the girl never sees because it is turned over to a pimp who is forcing her into the business—the girl can actually be considered a criminal. In some cases, for example, if the girl is convicted under a crimes against nature law, she can find herself labeled a registered sex offender and receive a far stiffer sentence than her john.

Most supporters of anti–sex offender policies don't have minor prostitutes, let alone the average sexually active teen, in mind. Many are simply shell-shocked by horrific tales of child molesters and are terrified that a predator may strike at random. Cases like those of Jaycee Lee Dugard (kidnapped at 11 and kept captive for 18 years by a known sex offender), Elizabeth Smart (abducted at 14 and sexually assaulted by a religious fanatic over a period of many months), and Shawn Hornbeck (snatched from his bicycle at 11, also by a sexual predator, and held for five years before escaping) are so horrifying that many people simply want to pass laws allowing us to just lock up the perpetrators and throw away the keys. But while such cases are gruesome, they really aren't common. This is hard to remember when the news media, politicians, and TV shows like *America's Most Wanted* (just ending a 23-year run) and *To Catch a Predator* (recently returning after a three-year hiatus) make it seem as if there is danger lurking around every corner. Add to this the fact that no criminals are more vilified than are sex offenders, and you can see how easy it has become to target anyone—no matter how young—who is involved in any behavior identified as a sex crime. This is true even if the illegality of the crime in question is, well, questionable.

It's not that real sex offenders don't exist, or that teens can't commit brutal sex crimes. But the way our legal system treats sex does little to address the real risks. In reality, the majority of sex crimes against children are committed by an adult who is known to the child. The US Department of Justice reports that 73 percent of rape victims know their assailants. For victims under 18, that number rises to an astonishing 93 percent. Additionally, a 2009 study conducted by the National Institute of Justice and Rutgers University found that the ever increasing laws requiring sex offender registration, residency restrictions, and mandatory minimum sentencing for sex crimes have not made a difference in preventing sex crimes against children. These crimes, if New Hampshire's Crimes Against Children Research Center is to be believed, are actually decreasing. This think tank discovered that between 1993 and 2005, the rate of reported child sexual abuse fell 40 percent.

But studies like these are ignored by terrified community members and by lawmakers who want to look tough on crime. So, rather than fighting to revamp the system, many people argue for more and more regulations. When these pass, the pool of those affected increases, and legislation designed with hardened criminals in mind gets applied to teens whose activities are significantly less threatening. To complicate matters further, state sex offender laws can trump juvenile offender laws (which generally result in milder penalties, shorter sentences, and sealed records). Moreover, our constitutional guarantee of states' rights has resulted in numerous situations where a sexually active teen may be doing something that is legal in one part of the country but criminal in another. It is little wonder, then, that minors have found themselves sitting in jail, or saddled with lifetime sexual offender status, for behaviors they honestly didn't know were crimes.

Think about it in this way: if we assume that kids are too immature to consent to have sex or to view pornography, then how can we possibly turn around and say those same kids have to be held to adult standards when they post a naked picture of themselves online or have sex with a slightly younger peer? Yet in many cases that is exactly what our legal system does. Hypocrisy about teens and sex is nothing new. Continuing to legislate contradictions into law without batting an eye is something else.

Love Grenade
Lidia Yuknavitch

When I first met Hannah in graduate school I was a woman gone numb. I would do anything. Anytime. Anywhere.

Hannah was one of those lesbians who looks like a beautiful boy—hazel eyes, that cool short curtain of hair hanging over one eye, broad shoulders, little hips, barely-there titties. More like M&M's. Hannah played basketball and softball and soccer when she wasn't being a Eugene lesbo and English grad student. She used to wait for me by my blue Toyota pickup truck between classes and hijack me and drive me to the coast, where we'd stay up all night getting it on in the back of my truck, drinking Heinekens and waiting for the sun to come up. Then we'd drive back and go to class. Or I would—Hannah thought grad school was kind of lame. She much preferred sex and club dancing.

So when Hannah captured me and my best friend, Chloe, in the hall after our 18th-Century Women Writers seminar, grabbing our wrists and pulling us toward the wall, I already knew it would be something sly. She smiled her sly Hannah smile and whispered, "Wanna go to the coast? I got us a room."

Chloe blinked so blankly her eyes looked like a doll's, and I think I coughed academically. But I have to admit it—my crotch went messy pretty much that instant.

Chloe said something about not having enough money or time, and anyway didn't we have seminar papers due?—to which Hannah said, patting Chloe's head like a puppy dog, "Don't worry, I already bought us the weekend, complete with a *kitchenette*," making Chloe smile as if she'd just eaten chocolate. I said something equally lame-ass, like I have to see what's up with my boyfriend (I have to see what's up with my *boyfriend*?), to which Hannah replied, "Really? Is he your *dad*?" and reached underneath the waist of my jeans with her thumbs. Hannah picked at something on the front of my shirt until I looked down like a 12-year-old fucktard and she tweaked my nose, laughing a little Hannah laugh, and then somehow we were on our way to Albertson's to load up the back with beer and wine and food.

We cleaned out my monthly food stamps buying Gruyère cheese and pickled herring and smoked salmon and those cool not-American chocolate bars with fruit ooze in the center and baguettes, the checkout lady scowling at us like somebody's mother. And, me being me, we also scored three great filet mignon steaks I stuffed in my pants. To try and recover some semblance of coolness.

Listen, you probably think you wouldn't, but I'm telling you, if Hannah said get in my truck we're going to the coast, raising her little trickster eyebrow and putting her hand right underneath your breast and against your first couple of ribs, going, *I dare you*, you'd go.

So there we were, crammed three-way up front in a pickup truck, beers at our ankles, Hannah at the wheel, Chloe in the middle looking a little like our kid, and me with my mane of blond out the window yelling wooooooo-hooooo. Chloe kept squirming between us. I mean, she was talking like normal and laughing like normal but her eyes had little electrical sparks in the corners. I kept looking at her but she kept looking away, or into the rearview.

About Chloe. We met each other in a Women's Studies class and hit it off right away. She was smart as a whip but not kiss-assy women's studies smart—her questions always burrowed underneath the obvious and her seminar papers were more thoughtful than mine. A lot. Not only were her eyes the deepest chocolate you've ever seen, but her tits were the roundest and fullest, most beautiful tits I've ever seen. When I first met her I assumed she was a dyke, mostly because she didn't have a boyfriend and her hair was cut in a boy haircut and she knew so much about women writers. Also, after about a year we shared a graduate teaching fellow office together and sucked some quite serious face. So we were definitely headed for—something.

That's a lie. I mean, it's not a lie—it's just that I'm telling it as if what was best about her was her hotness. I wish I could go back and tell her how intelligent and beautiful she was. I wish I had been able to understand the two best things about her—that she was loving, and that she was kind. But you don't get to go back and tap yourself on the shoulder and go, *Hey, fucktard. There's something big here.* I was busy dramatizing my sexuality.

In the truck with Hannah we were headed for the See Vue Inn. If you've never been, you are missing a lez secret hideaway. It's located on a bluff above a beach full of agates, fossils, and tide pools. Whales migrate within view and sea lions play in the surf. Elk, eagles, and deer are frequent visitors. But that's not why women go.

Women go because of the themed rooms. The Secret Garden Suite (private garden). The Crow's Nest (nautical). The Salish (Native American). Princess and the Pea (weirdly medieval). Mountain Shores (rustica). Far Out West (cowgirl). The Cottage (you get the "house" to yourself).

We had The Cottage.

But halfway there Chloe had to pee, so we stopped at a ratty little gas station in the coast range between Eugene and Florence. Peeing women trigger other women's bladders, so I went into the bathroom with Chloe. Those gas station bathrooms are squalid dumpholes that smell like someone shit air freshener. The floors always have weird black slime on them, the sinks are always stained with something that looks a little like a serial killing, and more often than not the toilet is backed up with either toilet paper or, well, you know. Miraculously, our toilet was not backed up. I tried to break open the crappy machine with the tiny sex toys in it like French Ticklers—no doubt installed for truckers—while Chloe peed.

When it was my turn, as I peed, I looked up and asked her, "Everything okay?"

"Yeah," she said.

"Then why are you scratching your mole?" I wiped up and flushed, looking back to see if the water was going down or coming back up at me.

Chloe went to look in the mirror—the glass made her face look kind of Special Olympics. She messed with her hair, pushing her bangs one way, then the other. Her face started to go red.

"Um, are you *sure* you are okay?" I asked.

When she turned around her eyebrows were knitting across

her forehead. Then she blurted out, "NO. I am NOT okay. Okay?" Her voice had a tinge of I'm a grown woman trying not to cry in it.

I sat back down on the toilet, which was making a high-pitched water-pipe screeching sound. "What's up?" I asked.

She closed her eyes. She took a breath and held it in. I hate to say it, but she kind of looked like a Muppet there for a second. I said her name out loud. Then she spilled it.

"I've never licked pussy."

"What?" I said, as if I'd gone deaf.

I sat there staring at her. I looked at the ceiling, the floor with the black slime, then back at her. Was she nervous about having sex with women? It suddenly occurred to me that this was not something I ever thought about. And the reason I didn't think about distinctions such as this is that I was using my body as a sexual battering ram. On anyone and anything available. In fact, you might say I sexualized my entire existence at that point. It seemed to work a lot like alcohol and drugs. If you did it enough, you didn't have to think or feel anything but *mmmm, good.*

I looked at Chloe more playfully. "I thought that's what graduate school was for? I thought that's why we took Women's Studies? I thought all women did women in grad school so they could say I did a woman in grad school?" I laughed. I was kidding but kind of not.

"Shut up!" she spurted at me from her corner of the shithole. "It's not funny! I feel sick to my stomach!"

This threw me. "Like you're gonna barf? But why?"

She turned around in a circle or two, scratching her mole vigorously. "I just..."

"You just what?"

"I'm just afraid I'm going to—you know, like, gag or something."

"You're afraid you are going to gag?" I started laughing. I couldn't help it.

"Shut the fuck up!" She stomped her foot and made fists. I swear.

"Look," I said. "Calm the fuck down. I'm no bona fide lesbian—" This was indeed true. In Eugene at that time, anyway, if you were with women but you also, dang it, still liked the poke, you couldn't really be a card-carrying member. "—but I've been getting it on with women since I was fourteen and, you know, there's ... there's lots of stuff to do."

She considered this.

Then I said, "Besides, even if you did gag, gagging could be, you know, sorta cool, too, couldn't it?" I couldn't help myself. I started laughing again. She began to swear at me and kind of fake-slap my head, so I reached over and grabbed at her pants. "I'm going to do you right now, you coy little minx," I yelled, unbuttoning her pants and pulling them down. "Jesus. Your underwear is pink. People still wear pink underwear?"

But instead of laughing or swearing at me, she just stood there with her pants down. I looked at her. She looked at me. Then I said, "Do you want me to? I mean, for real?" She shook her head up and down. She closed her eyes.

Women all taste different. Her taste I'd say was a cross between kelp and heavy cream, plus a little hint of pee on the palate since we'd just peed. She smelled like hay and skin lotion. Partway through my lip smacking she said, "Okay. Stop. Let me try you."

I said, "Okay, but did that feel okay?" She laughed. I took that as a yes. Secretly I was glad she wanted to switch because my knees on that nasty floor grossed me out. I dropped my pants. She stared at me. I wasn't wearing underwear at all. "What?" I said. When she got down there and began her mouth-to-mouth I had to lean up against the wall to take the force of her. I laughed and said, "Well, jeez, for someone who has never done this, you are a natural."

From within her wet suction she said, "Shalty. Ish okay. Ish mmrowlrm good." Then she looked up and said, "Um, you kind of smell like filet mignon."

"Yeah," I said. "There's *lots* of other stuff to do, too, you know." I didn't think I was going to hit the high note on this one so I treated the whole incident as a teaching opportunity.

Then I heard a weird noise like the wall was being rammed. Chloe shot up and I turned around, and yep, there was Hannah's head up at the shitty little prison window on the wall. She was grinning and her fingers were curled over the railing—no doubt she'd hoisted herself up boy style.

"Whatcha doing?" she said. And laughed her Hannah laugh.

By the time we got to The See Vue, there were three of us in the car who had licked pussy. Tragedy averted. Minimal gagging.

Our little cottage sported a fireplace, so I said don't do anything without me and drove off to get firewood. When I got back, the door was open. I went in. The two of them were in bed with the covers pulled up just underneath their tits—Hannah's M&M's and Chloe's glorious pendulous globes—smiling like Cheshire cats. Cheshire cats who had licked pussy. And in the middle of the bed was a little suitcase that Hannah brought—filled with toys.

I immediately dropped the wood on the floor, shut the door, and stripped, launching myself onto the bed like Superwoman.

Whoever was staying in the Princess and the Pea or the Salish or the Far East, they must've gotten an earful. Hours of woman on woman on woman whose regular lives didn't allow for such wild abandon. Sometimes Hannah's fist up my cunt, Chloe's mouth on mine or me sucking her epic tits. Sometimes Hannah on her stomach, me up her ass with a strap-on, Chloe behind me giving me a reach-around—a skill she intuited. Sometimes Chloe on all fours, me and Hannah filling every hole licking every mouth rubbing her clit making her scream making her entire corpus shiver her head rocking back her woman wail let loose gone primal cum and shit stains and spit and tears. I came in Hannah's mouth, her face between my legs like some goddess in a new myth. Chloe came with Hannah's fingers in her ass and pussy, her body convulsing and falling off the bed, me wrapped around her and laughing and hitting my head on the wall. Hannah came while jamming a dildo up herself as I buried my face in the clit of her. She pulled my hair. She pushed my head. Chloe curled under me licking and gagging but not not not stopping. I don't know how many times we came—it seemed unending.

We ate each other we ate pickled herring we ate Gruyère cheese. We ate the animal out of each other's bodies we ate steak we ate chocolate two women my chocolate. We drank each other we drank all the beer we drank all the wine we peed outside. We got high on skin and cum and sweat we got high on pot. We came in waves we ran out and into the waves.

I wanted to stay like that forever—outside of any "relation-ship" I had ever had and inside the wet of an unnamed sexuality. The moon a grand spectator. As full of alive as the ocean outside the door. All the night it was difficult to tell whose body was whose. The woman of it drowned me. It nearly cleaved my mind. And again. Again. Waves.

In the morning we wrapped ourselves in blankets and drank

coffee and perched ourselves about. Hannah on the porch railing outside and Chloe in a big overstuffed chair in the main room and me back in the bed curled up like a lion who'd just eaten a baby. It would have made a nice photo, three women contented like that, three women waking from their own pleasure without anyone or anything to put them back in their clean and proper places. But life is life.

On the beach later that day Hannah grabbed Chloe's hands and swung her around ring-around-the-rosy style, harder and harder. Chloe was laughing and then the wind and rain kicked up and then Hannah swung her too hard and let go and Chloe went tumbling over sand and rock and scraped the shit out of her face and shoulder. Also she wrenched her back.

Back in the cottage, I smoked a great deal of please-don't-let-this-all-go-to-hell pot and got so high I passed out at 8:00 p.m. When I awoke, Chloe was sitting on the floor in front of the fireplace crying and Hannah was nowhere to be seen. When she came back to the cottage we were just three women again, living women lives, me with a boyfriend and Chloe with a seminar paper due and Hanna just standing there with her idea that had gone to shit. On the solemn heavy drive home I got pulled over and given a ticket by some man cop—a little piece of paper that might as well have read: *Not so fast, ladies.*

I don't know why women can't make the story do what they want.

I don't.

I don't know why the story of a woman's sexuality can't be the next Great American Novel. Form coming from content.

When we got back to our ordinary lives, Chloe told me she was in love with me. A sentiment I couldn't find in myself to return, hard as I tried. I wish I could go back and try. It was real, what she offered. But kindness wasn't something I even recognized. Hannah's girlfriend tried to commit suicide, feeling betrayed and alone. Though I had an episode or two left with Hannah, I was seduced away from her wild abandon eventually by a man with a fifth of whiskey, and like Faye Dunaway in *Barfly,* I followed him toward the meated smell and taste of poke.

Pottymouth
Kevin Sampsell

You can't judge a mouth by the shade of its lipstick. Sometimes the girls you imagine would talk the dirtiest in bed turn out to be the most offended when you grunt something about how they should push their tits together, while it turns out that nice girl who always wears the long-sleeve turtleneck wants you to "spray it" on her face. I like girls who break the stereotype in that way— the bad good girl. But whether you're dating a girl or merely adding to your booty-call roster, you must scramble to adapt to their semantics. Their love language.

After years of research, I have compiled some case studies.

The girl who ran away from home as a teen, whose father is a cop, and exhibits reckless behavior: Christy introduced me to the concept of oral sex; I was ignorant of the possibility that men could go down on women until I was 18. We woke up together at a friend's apartment. She asked if I wanted to eat her out. Flustered and grossed out, I said no, thanks. The next time we were together, she stole a line from Prince and said, "I sincerely want to fuck the taste out of your mouth." I was intimidated by her and almost lost my erection, even at an age when it was impossible for me not to have an erection. "Fuck me harder, baby," she said, in an attempt to soothe and encourage. A few minutes later she lost patience and screamed, "Pound my fucking twat!"

The girl who is still close to her parents, has various pets that sleep with her, likes to imagine that she is "one of the boys," but often kills the mood when she's around: Beth said she would leave me if I spoke the word *cunt* in front of her. I asked politely if I could say *pussy*, but she didn't like that either. We had our sex in silence. Once, when I tried to add even the blandest vocal dynamics, mid-fuck—"Does that feel good?"—she had a meltdown and asked if I was trying to humiliate her. She also would not let me pet her animals unless I was clothed.

The girl who is too self-involved to ask you about yourself, dances ballet but likes angry rap music, joins organizations like PETA and Greenpeace but loses interest in them quickly: Whitney never once mentioned my cock or my eagerly darting tongue, but focused on her own goodies whenever we screwed around on her ridiculously large bed. "Doesn't my pussy feel good?" she would ask me. "Yes," I would pant, trying to fuck her good enough so she'd notice me. "I'm the best fuck in the mall, ain't I?" she'd query (we were working in a mall at the time). Once, in a moment of generosity, she said, "If you make me come, I'll make you come, too." She must not have realized that I already came and was merely working overtime until some tension left her body.

"Feed on my titties," she said. "I wanna hear you slurp."

The girl who doesn't own a television, likes (and understands) poetry, sometimes gets blind drunk and loses her cell phone at lesbian bars: Jen was basically a sex machine who would suck or hump anything that limped. She had a loud voice and talked constantly, even with her mouth full. She would suck my cock first thing in the morning while talking about her fucked-up dreams. Strangely, she always referred to our body parts in proper clinical terms: "Your penis turned into a hammer (lick, pause) and you were nailing me to a cross, and then (suck, head twist, lick) your hands turned into penises and you fucked my vagina (lick, pause) with your left hand while titty-fucking me (suck) with your right." When she got drunk, she liked to turn the tables. "How 'bout I fuck you tonight?" she'd slur. "I got a strap-on with your rectum's name on it. You wanna be my sexy bitch tonight?"

The girl with enormous breasts whose parents were hippies: When I first slept with Blossom, she told me that sex was the best drug, the "highest high." She would move up and down on me, making wild animal noises, as I lay on my back. Then she'd laugh unself-consciously and raise her arms as if she was worshipping some wacky moon goddess. She smelled like cinnamon and said things like, "When you come, it's like you're painting my soul." And I would try to match her with my own woo-woo hoo-ha: "Your tits are like beautiful planets that I want to explore and write poems about. Your pussy is the most delicious pomegranate."

The just-divorced girl with an exotic accent: I wasn't really sure where she was from (maybe Australia, maybe Oklahoma), but the sound of her voice made me hard in my pants, even when she was talking about how she and her ex-husband had sex every day for nine years. Sometimes more than once. Before she moved "back home" (wherever that was), she spent her last night in town at my place. She called me by her ex's name a few times but didn't apologize (she had downed the last of my liquor). She wanted me to speak Spanish to her but I didn't know any. She told me a few key phrases: *Se siente rico*: "That feels good." *Te voy a echar de menos*: "I am going to miss you." *Ajustado culo*: "Tight ass." I wanted to impress her, but I was saying the words wrong and then I ejaculated too soon. "I'm sorry," I told her, "that wasn't my best." I felt like an athlete who had just choked in a winnable game. "It was good," she said. "You fucked me good." We were drunk and falling asleep but I felt bad. "You're just saying that," I said.

About the Contributors

RADLEY BALKO is a writer and investigative journalist in Nashville, Tennessee. He now writes for *Huffington Post*, formerly for *Reason* magazine. Balko's reporting is credited with freeing a Mississippi man from death row. In 2011 he was named the L.A. Press Club's Journalist of the Year.

GRETA CHRISTINA is one of the most widely read, well-respected bloggers in the atheist blogosphere. She is a regular atheist correspondent for AlterNet; she has been published in *Ms., Skeptical Inquirer,* the *Chicago Sun-Times*, and more; and she has been writing for her own *Greta Christina's Blog* since 2005. Find her at www.freethoughtblogs.com/greta.

TRACY CLARK-FLORY is a staff writer at Salon.com, where she covers sex, love, and relationships. Her personal essay "In

Defense of Casual Sex" was selected for the anthology *Best Sex Writing 2009.*

A biomedical engineer by training, **ADRIAN COLESBERRY** works in pharmaceutical manufacturing by day and, in the evenings, writes dirty, funny, dirty books and does stand-up comedy, proving again the age-old formula: corporate drug manufacturing + time (approx. 2 hours) = comedy.

AMBER DAWN is a writer, filmmaker, and performance artist based in Vancouver. She is the author of the novel *Sub Rosa* (Arsenal Pulp Press, 2010), editor of the Lambda Award–nominated *Fist of the Spider Woman* (Arsenal Pulp Press, 2008) and co-editor of *With a Rough Tongue: Femmes Write Porn* (Arsenal Pulp Press, 2005).

CAMILLE DODERO is a staff writer at the *Village Voice.*

TIM ELHAJJ's work has appeared in the *New York Times, Brevity, Guernica*, and other publications. He edits the online journal *Junk: a literary fix.* Tim's first book, *Dopefiend: A Father's Journey from Addiction to Redemption,* is forthcoming from Central Recovery Press in October 2011.

ELLEN FRIEDRICHS is a health and sexuality educator (and mom) based in New York City, where she teaches high school and college classes and runs About.com's GLBT Teens website. Ellen has contributed to previous editions of *Best Sex Writing*, and has written for Alternet.org. Nerve.com, Babble.com, gURL. com, the *Jewish Daily Forward*, and *Nature Medicine.* Find her at www.sexEdvice.com.

ROXANE GAY's writing appears or is forthcoming in *Best New Stories from the Midwest 2011, NOON, Cream City Review, Black Warrior Review, Brevity, McSweeney's Internet Tendency,* The Rumpus, and many others. She is an *HTMLGIANT* contributor, co-edits *PANK*, and her first collection, *Ayiti*, will be released in 2011. She has a website.

LYNN HARRIS (www.lynnharris.net) is an award-winning journalist, author, and novelist, as well as co-creator of the award-winning website BreakupGirl.net. She is now the communications specialist for Breakthrough, a transnational organization that creates pop culture to promote human rights.

DR. MARTY KLEIN is a licensed marriage and family therapist and certified sex therapist. He is the author of six books about sexuality, including the award-winning *America's War on Sex* and the forthcoming *Sexual Intelligence: What We* Really *Want from Sex, and How to Get It.* He blogs at www.MartyKlein.com.

AMANDA MARCOTTE is a writer, prominent citizen of the Internet, and feminist gadfly. She has written for Slate, *The American Prospect, Bitch, The Nation*, and Salon, among other publications.

JOAN PRICE (www.joanprice.com) is the author of *Better Than I Ever Expected: Straight Talk about Sex after Sixty* and *Naked at Our Age: Talking Out Loud about Senior Sex*, both from Seal Press. Visit her award-winning blog about sex and aging: www.NakedAtOurAge.com.

TRACY QUAN's latest novel is *Diary of a Jetsetting Call Girl*. Her debut, *Diary of a Manhattan Call Girl*, is an international best seller.

A frequent contributor to The Daily Beast and other publications, she offers advice about love at ExpertInsight.com. Her website is www.TracyQuan.net.

THOMAS ROCHE's first novel, *The Panama Laugh*, is a noir-themed zombie apocalypse. Sadly, his political commentary strays far too often into the same territory. He is a member of the training staff at San Francisco Sex Information. His recent writing can be found at TinyNibbles.com, Techyum.com, WriteSex.Net, Night-Bazaar.com, and Thomasroche.com.

KEVIN SAMPSELL is the author of a memoir, *A Common Pornography* (Harper Perennial) and the story collections *Creamy Bullets* (Chiasmus Press) and *Beautiful Blemish* (Word Riot). He lives in Portland, Oregon, and runs the micropress Future Tense Books.

HUGO SCHWYZER teaches gender studies and history at Pasadena City College. His writing has appeared in the *Guardian*, Jezebel, Alternet, the *Los Angeles Times*, The Frisky, and at the Good Men Project. He is co-author, with Carre Otis, of *Beauty, Disrupted: A Memoir*. He blogs at www.hugoschwyzer.net.

KATHERINE SPILLAR is a founder and executive vice president of the Feminist Majority Foundation. Under her leadership as executive editor of *Ms.* (www.msmagazine.com, published by the Feminist Majority Foundation), *Ms.* increased its investigative reporting, winning the prestigious Maggie Award for its investigation into the network of antiabortion extremists connected to the murderer of Dr. George Tiller.

CHRIS SWEENEY is a freelance journalist who has written for the print and digital versions of *Playboy, Wired, Popular Mechanics,* and *DVM Newsmagazine,* among others. He was awarded a 2011 U.N. Foundation Global Health Journalism Fellowship, and holds a master's degree in journalism from Northwestern University.

ABBY TALLMER is a freelance writer from New York's West Village. "Losing the Meatpacking District: A Queer History of Leather Culture" is dedicated to the memory of Abby's good friend Saul Rubio, to the many others lost in their prime to AIDS during the first terrible decade of that disease, and to the memory of a New York City that artists could afford to live in.

RACHEL RABBIT WHITE is a New York City–based journalist writing in the beat of sex and gender. Follow her at http://rachel-rabbitwhite.com.

LIDIA YUKNAVITCH is the author of three books of short stories and a memoir, *The Chronology of Water* (Hawthorne Books, April 2011), as well as the forthcoming novel *Dora: A Head Case.* She has written for The Rumpus, *PANK,* The Nervous Breakdown, as well as regional and national literary journals and anthologies.

About the Editors

SUSIE BRIGHT (www.susiebright.com) is one of the world's most respected voices on sexual politics, as well as an award-winning and best-selling writer who has edited hundreds of the finest authors working in American literature and progressive activism today. She was a screenwriting consultant on *Bound, Erotique*, and *The Celluloid Closet*, and hosts the show "In Bed with Susie Bright" on Audible.com. Her most recent book is *Big Sex Little Death: A Memoir*.

RACHEL KRAMER BUSSEL (www.rachelkramerbussel.com) is a prolific author, editor, and blogger. She has edited over 40 books of erotica, including *Best Bondage Erotica 2011*; *Gotta Have It*; *Obsessed*; *Women in Lust*; *Her Surrender*; *Orgasmic*; *Bottoms Up: Spanking Good Stories*; *Spanked*; *Naughty Spanking Stories from A to Z* 1 and 2; *Fast Girls*; *Smooth*; *Passion*; *The Mile High Club*; *Do Not*

Disturb; *Tasting Him*; *Tasting Her*; *Please, Sir*; *Please, Ma'am*; *He's on Top*; *She's on Top*; *Caught Looking*; *Hide and Seek*; *Crossdressing*, and *Rubber Sex*. She is the series editor of *Best Sex Writing* and winner of six IPPY (Independent Publisher) Awards. Her work has been published in over one hundred anthologies.

Rachel wrote the popular "Lusty Lady" column for the *Village Voice* and is a sex columnist for SexisMagazine.com. Rachel has written for *AVN*, *Bust*, Cleansheets.com, *Cosmopolitan*, *Curve*, The Daily Beast, Fresh Yarn, theFrisky.com, Gothamist, *Huffington Post*, Mediabistro, *Newsday*, the *New York Post*, *Penthouse*, *Playgirl*, *Radar*, the *San Francisco Chronicle*, *Time Out New York*, and *Zink*, among others. She has appeared on *The Martha Stewart Show*, *The Berman and Berman Show*, NY1, and Showtime's *Family Business*. She hosted the popular In the Flesh Erotic Reading Series (www.inthefleshreadingseries.com), and speaks at conferences, does readings, and teaches erotic writing workshops across the country. She blogs at www.lustylady.blogspot.com.

A version of "Criminalizing Circumcision: Self-Hatred as Public Policy," by Marty Klein, was originally published at Sexual Intelligence (sexualintelligence.wordpress.com). "The Worship of Female Pleasure," by Tracy Clark-Flory, was originally published at Salon (Salon.com), May 21, 2011. "Sex, Lies, and Hush Money," by Katherine Spillar, was originally published in *Ms.*, Summer 2011 issue. "The Dynamics of Sexual Acceleration," by Chris Sweeney, was originally published in *Playboy*, January 2011 issue. "Atheists Do It Better: Why Leaving Religion Leads to Better Sex," by Greta Christina, was originally published at Alternet (alternet.org), May 17, 2011. "To All the Butches I Loved between 1995 and 2005: An Open Letter about Selling Sex, Selling Out, and Soldiering On," by Amber Dawn, was originally published in *Persistence: All Ways Butch and Femme*, edited by Ivan E. Coyote and Zena Sharman (Arsenal Pulp Press, 2011). A version of "I Want You to Want Me," by Hugo Schwyzer, was published at The Good Men Project (http://goodmenproject.com/), February 2011. A version of "Grief, Resilience, and My 66th Birthday Gift," by Joan Price, was originally published in *Naked at Our Age: Talking Out Loud about Senior Sex*, by Joan Price (Seal Press, June 2011). "Latina Glitter," by Rachel Rabbit White, was originally published at SexIs Magazine (sexismagazine.com). "Dating with an STD," by Lynn Harris, was originally published (as "Life with an STD") at Salon (www.Salon.com), January 17, 2011. "You Can Have Sex with Them; Just Don't Photograph Them," by Radley Balko, was originally published in *Reason*, February 28, 2011. "An Unfortunate Discharge Early in My Naval Career," by Tim Elhajj, was originally published (as "An Unfortunate Discharge") in *Guernica*, August 2010. "Guys Who Like Fat Chicks," by Camille Dodero, was originally published in the *Village Voice*, May 4, 2011. "The Careless Language of Sexual Violence," by Roxane Gay, was originally published at The Rumpus (www.therumpus.net), March 10, 2011. "Men Who 'Buy Sex' Commit More Crimes: *Newsweek*, Trafficking, and the Lie of Fabricated Sex Studies," by Thomas Roche, was originally published at Tiny Nibbles (www.tinynibbles.com), July 20, 2011. "Taking Liberties," by Tracy Quan, was originally published in *Marie Claire Malaysia*, June 2011. Reprinted with permission from *Marie Claire Malaysia* (www.marieclaire.com.my/). "Why Lying about Monogamy Matters," by Susie Bright, was originally published in *Susie Bright's Journal* (susiebright.blogs.com), March 8, 2011. "Penis Gagging, BDSM, and Rape Fantasy: The Truth about Kinky Sexting," by Rachel Kramer Bussel, was originally published at SexIs Magazine (sexismagazine.com). "Adrian's Penis: Care and Handling," by Adrian Colesberry, was originally published in *How to Make Love to Adrian Colesberry*, by Adrian Colesberry (Gotham, 2011). A version of "Love Grenade," by Lidia Yuknavitch, was originally published in *The Chronology of Water*, by Lidia Yuknavitch (Hawthorne Books, 2011). "Pottymouth," by Kevin Sampsell, was originally published in *Fanzine*, 2010.